Advance NOT to P

"Throughout history people have followed scouts who guided them where they needed to go: Christopher Columbus, Lewis and Clark and John Muir. These trailblazers faced and overcame challenges that gave others hope because they'd been there and back. Many times their wisdom and insight saved multitudes from going down paths that would only get them further off track. But even more importantly, their efforts and sacrifice found the best path to go, saving those following both time and unnecessary pain.

David & Caron Loveless's new book, 'Nothing To Prove' is filled with this type of invaluable insight. From the pain of their journey they guide the reader into the healing presence of a gracious and loving Creator. Having known them for 30 years, I have personally benefited time and again from the extraordinary wisdom God has given them. May the journey they share in 'Nothing To Prove' be a healing balm in your life as well."

FRANCIS ANFUSO
Pastor of Rock of Roseville, Sacramento, CA
and *author of 14 books, including "Perfectly Positioned"*

"'Darkness must be brought into the light in order for us to be healed. Secrets must be exposed to others for God to do his full work.' We have seen the Loveless' courageously and faithfully live these words as pilgrims and now practitioners for the sake of others. In a mere 118 pages, Caron and David delve into the depths of our souls by revealing their own.

'Nothing to Prove' is packed with vulnerability, raw courage and powerful tools for transformation. We will recommend this book as a discipleship resource in our own church and with the pastors and leaders we serve."

REV. CLARE AND REV. SCOTT LOUGHRIGE
Lead Co-Pastors, Crossroads Church & Ministries, Marshall MI

"I do not believe I have read a more profoundly important book in the last 20 years. 'Nothing To Prove' is a masterpiece! The crushing of David and Caron Loveless's lives produced brilliant diamond that should be viewed and treasured. I am not exaggerating! Read it and see. Please."

CLARK WHITTEN
Pastor of Grace Church
Author of "Pure Grace"

"David and Caron Loveless offer invaluable, and practical, insight in their new book, 'Nothing to Prove'. They directs us to, in my opinion, the most important, and rarely understood, barrier to our experience here on earth: our identity. David and Caron make the case that most of us are unaware of the implications of our own 'sincere delusion' when it comes to accurate thinking about our true identity. David couches all he describes in the context of his own raw failure, and how that he, and Caron, used that failure to fuel a deeper understanding and appreciation for their marriage. They end the book by drawing down theory into practical next steps that will improve your mental, emotional, and spiritual landscape"

BRENT SAPP
CEO & Founder of Inc. Navigator

"Someone has said, 'Never let success get to your head and never let failure get to your heart.' What David and Caron Loveless have done with honesty and courage in this book is reveal their personal journey into the first part of that quote and their remarkable journey of grace and forgiveness into the second part, together.

Many of us have been privileged to stand beside them with each remarkable step of recovery they've taken. Those steps are recorded in this book for the blessing and help of all who read. You will profit and be encouraged from the openness and honesty of their experience written down, as have I."

PAUL BURLESON
President, Vital Truth Ministries

"What would it mean to live as if we are enough, have enough and do enough? Surely it would be a life well lived. It would mean we are deeply anchored in our most true identity IN Christ. It would mean we are comfortable in our own skin. It would mean we are at peace with our abilities and successes as well as our limits and losses. It would mean we know how to engage in our relationships is healthy and satisfying ways.

If this is the kind of life you long to live more fully then this is the book for you. David and Caron offer clear and compelling steps that lead to a transformed life. Because they are brutally vulnerable about their relational challenges and failures their book has a depth and perspective that is hard to find. Live what they have written and you will find you are **living more fully alive!**"

JAMES COFIELD
Professional Counselor/ Soul Care Provider
Co-author of The Relational Soul

NOTHING
to PROVE

*Find the satisfaction and significance
you've been striving for at the
core of your true identity*

David & Caron Loveless

LIVE TRUE PUBLISHING

LIVE TRUE PUBLISHING

Nothing To Prove

Contents

Introduction

This is going to be a pretty bold statement, but it's absolutely true. Of all the teaching and messages we've heard, conferences and seminars we've attended and books we've digested over the course of our lives, what we're about to share with you has done more to bring about personal transformation than all of those put together. It has saved our marriage. And, it's not a stretch to say, it may have even saved one of our lives.

Whatever route you took to get to this book, whether it was from our blog or podcast, social media or a friend's recommendation, we're glad you're here. And, whatever emotional, spiritual or relational shape you're in right now, we're confident there is something vital for you in the pages of this book.

We are telling our story for four reasons:

- To help you avoid some of the train wrecks, heartaches and headaches we have experienced

- To bring hope and direction if you are currently experiencing failure, loss, discouragement or disappointment

- To offer a real way out of the exhaustion, frustration, stress and anxiety our culture believes should be normal

- To show you how to live more passionately fulfilled and powerfully anchored from the core of your true identity.

With brutal honesty we walk you step-by-step through our own life changing process and pass on to you all the help, wisdom and ah-ha's we've experienced that have the potential to bring unprecedented transformation in your own personal and professional life. Like someone has said, "We can't take our life back, but we can pay it forward."

As we go along we'll ask you key questions to help locate where you are now and what might be currently holding you back from the ultimate satisfaction and significance you desire. We'll talk about a shift in awareness that needs to take place. Then we'll share some of the practices we use that can fuel and strengthen your ability to live more consistently from your true self.

If just some of the lessons we've learned the hard way can bring you increased personal awareness, spiritual growth and better emotional and professional balance, our time and effort in writing this book will have been totally worth it.

As you read, if you have questions, don't hesitate to contact us. You can reach us on our **Live True Facebook Page** or feel free to email us at **david@youlivetrue.com** or **caron@youlivetrue.com**, or you can find us at **http://www.youlivetrue.com**.

Step #1

Pinpoint what drives your compulsive identity

We all have a significant, driving force inside us, a central steering system in our head that challenges, accuses, directs, corrects and generally bullies us all day long.

If we can pinpoint what that system is, and where it's coming from, we can free ourselves from an internal slavery that keeps us bound and defeated in important areas of our lives.

If we don't locate this driver, it's usually just a matter of time before something starts breaking down, either relationally, professionally, emotionally, physically, financially, or spiritually.

Chapter 1

The Nightmare Awakening

*How ironic that the difficult times we fear might ruin us
are the very ones that can break us open
and help us blossom into who we were meant to be.*

Elizabeth Lesser

We sit next to each other on one side of a massive conference table. Stiff. Silent. Numb. We have just flown to Indiana and arrived at a strange office, in a strange town and we're about to start a one and a half day counseling session with two counselors we have never met.

Like a couple waking in the hospital after a massive train wreck, we feel as dazed and confused as any marriage has after the harsh floodlight of truth has suddenly exposed infidelity. Just weeks before this we were loving our lives and each other. We enjoyed kayak trips and bike rides together and felt honored to lead the large, vibrant church we had founded.

Then, the unthinkable happened. A hidden infidelity David had ended years earlier was leaked to several people.

When David discovered what had happened he immediately called a meeting with church elders. There, gasping with sobs, he made a full, gut wrenching confession. Then days later, after much sleeplessness and agony David resigned his position as senior pastor of the beloved congregation we had led for twenty-nine years. The leaders agreed this was best. And the horrific news was announced to the church and local newspaper. We had asked to speak to the church ourselves but the leaders felt that wasn't wise. So, we each wrote letters that were read to the congregation. Fervent prayers were lifted for our family and marriage and money was collected to help pay counseling expenses. David and Caron are permanently gone, the church was told, and they will not be allowed back.

Now, weeks later we sit exhausted, barely speaking. We're thinking, who just hijacked our lives? We had lost our income, our spiritual community, most of our friends, our international ministry relationships, our reputution, and, before long, we would also lose our home. In a bleary-eyed fog we wait for our session to start. It couldn't have felt more foreign than if we'd been grabbed by aliens and dropped in the Twilight Zone.

Across the table, our counselors, Rich and Jim, sit ready to listen. They see clients as a team. Most of the time, Jim takes notes and Rich asks questions. Their faces reflect the gravity of our situation. There's a flipchart with a diagram at the end of the table and they've already studied the assessments and questionnaires we filled out before we came.

"David, what we need to figure out here," Rich says, "is what made you so vulnerable, that you chose this unfortunate way of coping with your life."

"On the surface, we have the obvious. This is a tragic, devastating situation, especially for you, Caron. Words don't do it justice. We know that. At the moment, your marriage is unrecognizable. We're going to deal with that. Though your marriage is in trouble, it is not the real problem here.

The real problem is deeper. And it has been driving a lot of your behavior all of your life. As we unpack your stories we believe you're both going to see ways you've been functioning with certain hidden, internal beliefs that have sabotaged the way you worked, handled stress and related to each other at the time all this happened. Though we don't often hear about it, everyone carries similar beliefs and it causes us all to do some pretty dumb stuff sometimes. You guys can get through this. But you're going to have to be willing to feel and hear some things that may be difficult to accept about the way you've been processing your lives."

Chapter 2

What We Know Now

*You can never be other than who you are
until you are willing to embrace the reality of who you are.*
David Benner

You don't have to experience a tragedy like ours, or any other failure with a thousand different names, in order to identify the real root of your own internal issues. We hope it won't come to that. Our purpose in writing this book is to help you avoid some of the same ditches in your future, if possible. Unfortunately, for many of us it often does take a serious trial, illness or loss to break us open enough to see parts of our lives that aren't working so well.

Each day, from the moment we wake up, to the time our heads hit the pillow we live out of a story we've come to believe about our selves. This storyline thrives in our mind's subconscious, which is why we're often unaware of many of our own self-defeating patterns of behavior. But just because you aren't aware of it, have no doubt, the "story of you" is alive and well and it powerfully affects everything you do, say and think about yourself, others and - most importantly - God.

This story, these hidden beliefs you hold about yourself are the basis for what you believe is your identity.

The 64,000 Dollar Questions

Before you read further, pause here and think about how you would answer these two questions.

1) If you remove your job, your roles, your gender, your relationships, your titles, your possessions, your degrees, your achievements and your failures... Who would you say that you are?

2) Without naming your family, the work you do, things you own, or a role you play in a primary relationship... How would you describe yourself to someone you've just met?

Who we truly think we are at our core will influence every decision and every reaction to every loss and every gain we ever have. It will affect our perceptions of random events, family members, lifelong friends, the work we do, the accomplishments we strive for and even the failures we experience. So, when you're alone and no one's looking, who do you really think you are?

We can't say this strongly enough. Who you believe you are at your deepest level impacts the quality and outcome of every part your life.

The Teachers Are Clueless

Looking back we thought we pretty much understood all we needed to know about our identities. After college, David had spent four years in seminary and through the years we had both given countless talks and messages about who the scriptures say we are in Christ. While what we taught was true---our experience and understanding had not gone far enough.

We were clueless about the most significant aspects of our "inborn identity." Later we were tempted to beat ourselves up about it. How did we not know some of this? But a wise person once said, "You can't know what you don't know."

After our world fell apart we needed a better way to know each other and ourselves. Some of our old ways of doing life had failed us. And, at the point of our greatest failure, we stumbled into what, for us, would be the "Eureka!" of a lifetime.

Through scripture, our story, great counseling and teaching plus our own hunger to know more, we are now daily practicing proven steps to a path that can help overcome much of the stress, anxiety, exhaustion and disillusionment you sometimes feel.

Whenever we share these concepts we see people begin to make internal shifts that profoundly impact the meaning, purpose, fulfillment, freedom, and enjoyment in their lives. And the more they practice the more benefits they report.

For us, where there was once frustration, discouragement, failure and incalculable loss, there has come a remarkable resurrection. Now we can even say it may have been worth the pain to gain the goodness.

Chapter 3

The Story We Tell Ourselves

*How crazy it is to be "yourself" by trying
to live up to an image you have unconsciously
created in the minds of others.*

Thomas Merton

Back in our counseling session, Rich says, "We asked you to write out the highs and lows from your early life. So, David, why don't you start? Talk a bit about your history."

"Well," David says, "I had a pretty good upbringing. Over the course of my life I feel like I've been fortunate to experience God's love as well as the love of my parents, my wife, our kids and my close friends. I did feel approved in their love. Much of the time it was deeply satisfying. I remember feeling encouraged and supported by both of my parents. There was peace in our home. I grew up in small towns where my dad was always the pastor of a church and I participated in ministry at an early age."

"How early?" Rich asks.

"Well, if you don't count the preaching club I started in the second grade, around age eleven I was doing things like leading the singing for an adult revival meeting. I was affirmed a lot in any ministry I did. Guest leaders who came to our church often pulled me aside and predicted I was going to do great things for God one day. As a teenager I planned and lead our church's youth meetings and choirs. My parents always seemed proud of this.

"That's great," Rich said, "and did you feel good about yourself?"

"Yes and no. I also remember a nagging feeling that some part of me didn't measure up. There was one guy in particular, I always felt in competition with. He was a good friend of mine. He always seemed smarter, faster, stronger, better looking and his family was pretty well off and well known in our town. My family always seemed to struggle financially. I guess somewhere along the way I came to believe some part of me was flawed, defective, not enough."

"What do you mean?" Rich asked.

"Well, I think whenever I perceived there was a gap between who I was and who other people expected me to be or I thought I should be, I felt I needed to do something or say something to try to prove myself worthy."

"That's interesting," Rich says. Then he gets up and goes to the flip chart at the end of the table and starts teaching.

"We all have an operating system, he says, a story that plays in our head all day long about who we are. That story... that script... that voice... seems to be on an endless loop. It's actually your ego or false self's interpretation of what you've experienced throughout your life. Some people call it your old nature. What few of us realize is that there is actually another operating system in us that was there first, our spirit, our true self. The goal of our ego's voice is to take charge of our mind, to stay in control. It will even drown out the voice of our spirit, if necessary, to keep the upper hand.

Our false self-voice, tries to masquerade as our true identity, and it can try to get us to exaggerate or to diminish the person we think we are. We are all born with a solid, eternal foundation, made in the image of God. But, over time, as we interact with our caregivers and get up and out in the world who we really think we are begins to take on a life of its own.

Some of the forms our false selves latch on to are the condemning, destructive voices of shame, fear, or guilt. These emotions interpret our stories for us, advise us about who we are and who we aren't. And they will tell us some pretty skewed versions of our value, our resources, and the fate of our destinies in the world-usually expanding it larger or shrinking it smaller than the actual truth.

Your false self will constantly barrage you with accusations about your body, your intelligence, your spirituality, your habits, your abilities, and your weaknesses. It will be negative and critical of your past; it will make fearful predictions for your future and lie to you about what's actually happening in the present."

Rich ends our first session with this:

"We are all wired with legitimate needs that can and should be met. But, often, those voices, our false stories, can create such a web of lies, demanding exhausting schedules, exaggerating expectations and increasing anxiety so much that we end up caving in to illegitimate or counterfeit ways of coping. But, at the time, they can seem like the best, or only, option for us."

Chapter 4

Sleepwalking on Autopilot

Following a spiritual path is deciding that the (negative) picture before you will no longer dictate the orientation of your mind.

Hugh Prather

We are all walking around as a mix of two identities. No wonder we spend so much of our lives confused about who we are. Our first identity is our created identity or **true self/God self**, the second is our **conditioned/ compulsive identity**, which some also call the false self, our ego, shadow self or old nature.

Let's unpack our conditioned/compulsive identity first.

When we trust the conditioned/compulsive part of ourselves and allow it to do the driving, it often takes us on detours in the direction of getting noticed or applauded, toward ambition or addiction or to fear of failure or loss. It likes to make us think whatever it's up to at any given moment is only in our best interest. Sometimes, that's true. But, more often, it is reacting and defending against some perceived fear, shame or guilt.

So, how does this part of our identity get so powerful?

Since you came into the world you have been hard at work on an internal construction project. Because it began in your formative moments of consciousness your conditioned/compulsive identity has become automatic, second nature to you.

This version of you started before you could reason or fully understand the environment you lived in. Using trial and error you did the best you could to get what you needed from your primary caregivers. And, after food and water, what you needed most from them was safety and security.

At some point, we all learn we must get creative in order to get what we need in our family of origin.

Most parents and caregivers do the best they can to love and care for their kids. For some children early care comes in a healthy consistent way that breeds comfort and security. For others, baby and toddler life is a mixed bag. Sometimes our caregivers were there for us; sometimes they weren't. Sometimes they were kind, sometimes abusive. Sometimes they were attentive and sometimes they were distracted.

What's important to know is whatever was going on in the life of our early caregivers directly affected their level of patience, involvement, nurture and protection of us...which had direct, long term impact on our sensitive, developing emotional memory.

We figured out how to "read" and relate to our primary caregivers in ways that made them most happy and, thereby, most benefited us. We studied their faces, tone of voice, their reactivity and their touch. All these cues and more reflected back to us, they informed us about how this person felt about us and who they thought we were. If the face of our earliest caregiver does not consistently reflect love and belonging, we may probably question, on some level, whether we are loved and we belong wherever we go for the rest of our lives.

Even though this "caregiver dance" happened eons ago this significant, primal relationship is still very much hardwired in your brain and affects your behavior and your thinking today, including the conversation in your head right now about this book.

Throughout your young life you kept building on the platform of your most significant relationships - always maneuvering, trying to figure out the safest, most significant ways to be around teachers, friends, strangers, etc.

There's nothing evil or carnal about our early ego/identity construction. It is necessary to create "the container" we must use to interact in the world. But it's when we start feeling the need to overcompensate in situations where we don't feel secure or significant that it starts to become a problem for us. Say, if we think we're missing something, like great hair, or ab muscles or a Ph.D. our compulsive identity will come up with some way to cover for us, to make it appear to others as if we do indeed have it all together.

Your Automatic Unconscious

Just how automatic is our compulsive identity? Check this out. Neuroscientists and psychologists tell us that approximately 95% of our behavior is automatic (sub-cortical/unconscious) and only 5% is consciously planned! Dr. Roy Baumeister, Professor of Psychology at Florida State University, wrote about this in The Journal of Personality and Social Psychology, 1998.

So, according to the guys who study this stuff we basically spend 90 plus percent of our day sleep walking on autopilot.

This alone brings further, significant meaning when Jesus said *"Father, forgive them for they know not what they're doing"* (Luke 23:34). He wasn't just talking about forgiving those who were killing him. This is also an invitation to true self-awareness for everyone who is oblivious to the reactive, hurtful, negative, unhealthy things they do.

How many times have you been driving your car and all of a sudden you look up and you've arrived at your destination but you have no idea how you got there? Where did you go? You left the present moment of driving to deal with something more important going on in your head. Your subconscious took you for a joyride.

This happens in a whole lot of areas of our lives all the time.

Our internal zombie hijacks our identity throughout the course of the day through:

- reoccurring thoughts and beliefs
- instantaneous emotional reactions
- involuntary physical sensations

These habitual patterns happen in our minds, our emotions, and our bodies, and they can act as constricting forces that choke out the true life force of our original created identities. These thoughts, beliefs and behaviors give us an extremely limited and distorted view of God, others and ourselves.

As you're trying to pinpoint the main driver of your compulsive identity one way to look for it is to see where you get most activated around three primary life questions:

- Am I enough?
- Do I have enough?
- Have I done enough?

Time Out

Before you read further take a few minutes right now and reflect on each of the three questions above. Then ask yourself:

Which question most resonates as an issue for me most of the time?

How we answer these questions dictates the primary way we view ourselves and how we try to get what we need in the world. All three of the questions will affect us at different times, but one of them will keep showing up repeatedly like the recurring theme music of our lives.

3 Root Questions
in Search of Our Identity

Who am I?
How much do I have?
What am I here to do?

Chapter 5

The Drive for Approval

The identity you think you are does not exist.
Hugh Prather

After a stretch break we continue our session and Rich, says, "We've studied your profiles and it appears you both wrestle with feelings of unworthiness... Of not being enough. But you approach it different ways. You're both strong, passionate leaders with a great deal of accomplishment and yet your responses show, below the surface, you feel something's missing. Caron, does this ring true?"

Caron shifts in her seat. "Yes, for me it does. But, I would never have said that about David. He has always been so confident and on top of things. Not easily discouraged. I've struggled with insecurity and inferiority. It hasn't seemed to matter how many successes I have or talents I try to master, internally I've still felt insufficient. Even with decades of unconditional love from David and our boys I just couldn't seem to get fully convinced of my value."

"So, you've always thought this?" Rich asks.

"Yes. My parents weren't expressive with affection. I knew they loved me. But, I always felt I missed out on getting whatever gives kids that internal boost of 'okay-ness.' My parents did the best they could. But, starting at age five our home life was unpredictable. There were divorces, several stepparents, my father died at thirty-four, and there were several significant periods of abandonment. I was always adjusting to some loss or change. I felt something was wrong with my family and something was wrong with me."

"That's a lot for a kid to handle," Rich says. "How did you manage that?"

"It was my life so I just pressed through it. As a kid I spent a lot of time walking on eggshells. I feared getting on my parents bad side."

"How about with David?"

"Just like with my parents, I hated to disappoint him. It would crush me to feel his disapproval."

"And God?"

"For years, I've clung to scriptures that say God loves me just as I am. I started going to church as a teenager. I owe everything to that church and to the youth group I attended, they were a lifeline for me. But, my experiences with God didn't always match my growing knowledge of the Bible, at least not enough to sustain me, emotionally."

"Can you think of any other ways approval has affected you?"

"Well, sometimes, if I thought things weren't going well in some area of our ministry, I got anxious that we might lose momentum or status as a church. For many years I was also on staff at our church. It was our lives, not just our jobs. We worked a lot as a team. And, like a mama bear, I kept my eye on everything. I made suggestions to David. Most of the time, he says he appreciated this, but there were times if he didn't share my urgency for an issue, or have time to quickly delegate it to someone I would stay uptight and persist until he either got angry and reacted or did something about it. Many things always seemed in critical mode for me."

"What about you, David?" Jim asks.

"Well, I know I'm really hard on myself if I feel I'm not measuring up. Usually, I'm a pretty positive guy but I can get worn down and discouraged if I'm seeing too many things I'm working on go south or have some appearance of failure. If a talk I gave was not at least a triple, I felt disappointed in myself. Failure of any kind has not been an option for me, personally or professionally. If things were going bad I would look for the silver lining and find a way to make it seem better than it actually was. I felt like that was good leadership. I do have a genuine gift of faith. I see now that I sometimes minimized failures and maximized success. I didn't mind if others messed up. I just wasn't allowed to."

"That must have been hard, not allowing yourself to be human."

"I didn't see it that way. But when you put it like that it does sound pretty crazy."

"Anything else?"

"Well, there were certain national leaders I really looked up. I knew I could be like them, if I just had enough time and resources. I believed I could do much of the good, big things they were doing for God. But I was always working on my motives for ministry. I really wanted them to be pure. And at the same time I was keeping tabs on these other guys and beating myself up or questioning God about why the same things weren't happening for me.

Sometimes, I'd take it personally when key friends, family, our elders, or Caron would point out weak areas in church. It ate at me that something about my leadership was deficient. So I kept trying new initiatives, always changing things up hoping to get the results those leaders I admired were getting. I see now, some of the time, it was my own need for the approval of a select group of people that kept me so driven and exhausted and, ultimately, led to my vulnerability to moral failure."

"Well guys," Rich says, taking a deep breath and leaning back in his chair, "We're really sorry you've ended up here and, at the same time, we're glad you're here. This is all really tough. It doesn't feel like it now but what's happened to you is actually a 'severe mercy.' What Jim and I want you to see is whenever we're striving to gain approval or to feel special or to be a success it's because we're trying to cover some shame we feel over not being enough. And sooner or later for most of us---all that's going to break down. It'll just be too much for us to keep juggling all those hoops. And that's when things hit the fan."

Chapter 6

I'm Not Enough

*After man had chosen suffering in preference to
the joys of union with God, the Lord turned suffering
itself into a way by which man could come
to perfect knowledge of God.*

Thomas Merton

How can we tell if our compulsive need for approval is at work? One
way is to listen for times our minds drop troubling or negative hints like,
"Why are you always swimming upstream? You just don't have what
it takes. Something is wrong with you." For most of us, some form of
negative self-talk goes on in us every day. And it's been happening since
the beginning...

*Now the serpent was more crafty than any of the wild animals the
Lord God had made. He said to the woman, "Did God really say, 'You
must not eat from any tree in the garden'?"... "You will not surely
die," the serpent said to the woman. "For God knows that when you
eat of it your eyes will be opened, and you will be like God, knowing
good and evil."*
Genesis 3: 1, 4-5

Earlier in Genesis we witness the beginning of a great, fulfilling relationship
between Adam and Eve and God. The man and woman felt wonderful
about themselves (very good in fact) until the tempter comes along
and says: "Aren't you missing something? Wouldn't you rather be God
than just a creation of God? Wouldn't you rather be like the parent here
instead of a mere child?"

The tempter's first act of business was to suggest to a fully God-formed and lavishly loved couple that who they knew themselves to be was not enough. And we have been falling for the same suggestions and deceptions ever since.

Every time we compare ourselves to anyone, we end up seeing some way that we fall short. When shame is talking, it has only one message but many applications. Basically, it says: "Something is defective, flawed, broken, wrong with you, face the facts."

Adam and Eve were made in the image of God. They contained and expressed all the goodness of who God was, in their own unique ways. They were already like God. They had come from God and were totally complete, lacking nothing. God had fully created them, provided for them and blessed them with all they would ever need and more.

true self

Then the tempter came tricking the couple into desiring something that was already fully theirs. Adam and Eve were valuable and loved at this moment, just as much as the day they had been created. But the enemy tried to get them to think God was holding out on them.

Here's what happens next:

> Then the eyes of both of them were opened, and they realized
> they were naked (the literal word here is 'shamed'); so they sewed
> fig leaves together and made coverings for themselves.
> **Genesis 3:7**

Something is definitely missing now.

We all have a legitimate, God-given need to feel like we're enough, that we are what God said at the very beginning - "very good." But when we're not experiencing that or not convinced of our goodness we will do something to compensate for the lack we feel.

"I need another 75 likes on my Facebook page or I'm nothing."
"I need my boss to say I'm doing a good job!"
"I want people to tell me how great I look."
"I want to be famous. I need more stage time."

"I want to be known as a go-getter"

"I need a lot of affirmation that I'm needed and special."

Here's the crazy thing: with all the various ways we strive to gain approval we are creating our own life-depleting, energy-draining, soul-sucking stress.

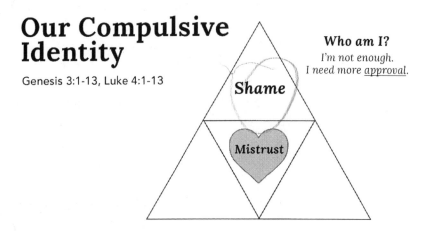

Our Compulsive Identity

Genesis 3:1-13, Luke 4:1-13

Who am I?
I'm not enough.
I need more <u>approval</u>.

Shame

Mistrust

The Gospel meets "I'm not enough"

The lie "I'm not enough" introduced in the garden also appeared at another important beginning, the start of Jesus' ministry.

The devil led (Jesus) to Jerusalem and had him stand on the highest point of the temple. "If you are the Son of God," he said, "throw yourself down from here. For it is written: 'He will command his angels concerning you to guard you carefully; they will lift you up in their hands, so that you will not strike your foot against a stone.'"
Jesus answered, "It says: 'Do not put the Lord your God to the test.'"
Luke 4:9-12

Satan seems to be telling Jesus: *"All you need to do is to jump off this high place, because we both know angels will allow you a safe landing. And when you do, the whole world will adore you. They will see how wonderful you are. Oh, and by the way, this will be much better for you than dying all alone on a cross with everyone hating you."*

Notice the identity question the tempter asks Jesus: *"If you are the son of God..."* He's casting doubt: *"Do you know who you really are?"* He's going after any remote chance that Jesus has a weak spot where he feels that he's not loved or doesn't belong or is not approved of.

Jesus had come to the desert straight from his baptism where he heard God confirm, "This is my Son, whom I love and in whom I am well pleased." The only approval that ultimately matters to Jesus is God's. Jesus knows for sure who he is and cannot be tempted to do something flashy because he doesn't need anyone else's approval.

Acceptance gives us a sense of belonging. And the value of our belonging is entirely dependent upon to whom we belong. Jesus' identity is already settled. He is the Son of God. He doesn't need the applause of the crowd, or the enemy, or even from his family and community.

Dr. Brene Brown has said, "The antidote to shame is love and belonging." Jesus centered his entire sense of love and belonging in God.

There is nothing wrong with getting approval. Where approval goes wrong is when we try to use it to compensate for our shame, to prove to ourselves and others that we are "very good."

Can there ever be enough approval? Every time someone admires us or compliments us, the experience rarely lasts. We want more. So we keep creating situations to get it. That can become pretty stressful, especially over many years. The results of accumulated stress can train wreck our health, emotional stability and important relationships.

What About You?

Before continuing, take a few minutes to reflect on the questions below. Do you:

- Talk up your accomplishments; talk a good game, always position yourself or your work in a better light than is fully true? Do you skew the facts to not look so bad or to look even better than they are? Do you often one-up others in conversations, meetings, while retelling a story? Have you been known to be competitive?

- Do you do lots of things for others often at the expense of your own needs or your family's needs? Do you volunteer a lot, or constantly work overtime to please the boss? Are you the responsible one everyone depends on? Do you resent not being noticed for all the good things you do for others?

- Do you stress about what to wear, over-focus on your clothes, your fitness, your teeth whitening, your sex appeal, your home, or parties and events you're planning? Are you attached to feeling special in some way? Is being unique and original most important to you?

- Do you boast in order to cover something about you that you feel isn't quite adequate or enough?

- How does it affect you when you see a competitor's picture in the paper or see a great picture of someone on the cover of a magazine?

- How do you feel when you remember a failure? When you consider your job title?

- What makes you feel most vulnerable? What makes you want to hide?

Now take a few minutes and think about how you answered the questions. Circle back to the ones that snagged or pricked something in you and ask yourself in the presence of God: "What is that about?"

But, what if you don't always relate strongly with the issue of shame and approval? There is another identity driver that creates its own kind of stress and anxiety.

Chapter 7

The Drive to Accumulate

Until we are prepared to accept the self we actually are, we block God's transforming work of making us into our true self that is hidden in God.

David Benner

Side Bar with David:

For much of our adult life, I have genuinely trusted that God would take care of all our needs. I didn't just teach about it, I was certain God promised to supply what we needed, and we have experienced his leadership and faithfulness in so many consistent, generous and even miraculous ways over the years. Tithing ten percent and more was a normal part of my life, a habit instilled in me by my parents. But still, there were times fear crept in when I thought we didn't have enough money in the bank. And I'd feel the urge to get creative, to come up with a plan to help God out.

Ever done anything like that?

In the past, fear stirred up a scarcity mentality and I ended up trying some "get rich quick schemes." I made some pretty stupid financial decisions that brought even more stress on me. Crazy, right? Here I am, craving less stress and more peace and, several key times, I put myself in financial situations that just shot the stress meter through the stratosphere.

Any time we entertain thoughts like "I don't have enough" it's going to bring an attack on our peace of mind, which directly impacts the health of our body. And sometimes, it'll cause us to go out and do things that drain our finances, damage our relationships or numb us to what is most true. Many years ago, I invested in the silver market because it seemed like a reasonably safe way to get ahead. We bought a bag of silver coins, stashed them in a secret place and before long the silver market plummeted.

Another time, I decided day trading was the way to go. We had three kids in a Christian school and creating a savings plan and retirement just wasn't happening for us. So, in the evenings I took courses and made a number of the recommended practice trades called "paper trades." And on paper I did pretty well. This boosted my confidence. So I did what we're never advised to do, and I borrowed some money in hopes of making more money. Everyone knows "it takes money to make money," right? I won some and lost some day trading, but in the end, I'm sad to say, we had to withdraw some equity from our home to pay back the debt I ended up owing.

Sidebar with Caron:

I've had some of my own "I don't have enough" fears. I like to keep things "just in case." I've been known to say, "You never know when I'm going to need this." If certain items went on sale at Costco or the art supply store I'd want to buy more than I needed because I was convinced I was saving money buying larger quantities. Greed comes from fear. Times like that I feared the money might not be there when I'd need those items later. And there is a certain pleasure in purchasing an appealing asset. But, it proves to be short lived. Right now, if you open our garage you'd see an abundance of bins on the shelves filled with unused craft and decorating supplies.

And I enjoy shopping. Sometimes I've even been aware enough to internally notice I am shopping to fill some other unnamed need. I go out for one item and come home with five or six. This is especially true if I'm shopping for clothes or home accessories. I love interior design. Beautiful things easily draw me in and I persuade myself "I really need this piece. If I don't get it now it won't be here when I come back later."

It was out of my love for design and the need for more space to host the church, our staff and other large gatherings, as well as our growing brood of grandchildren, that I convinced David to sell our 2,400 sq. ft. home and buy a larger fixer upper in a nice neighborhood. It had been on the market a long time, was the worst house in the subdivision and nothing had been done to update this early 1980's contemporary. I saw the potential and loved the challenge. It looked like a great investment. And with much delight I dove into a yearlong project overseeing the remodeling.

The result was stunning. I was so proud of how it turned out. But as much as I tried to keep costs down with savvy planning and purchasing the budget got out of control. We knew this would be the nicest home we would ever own so we excused some of our decisions thinking we would live in this home for the rest of our lives and share it generously with hundreds of people every year, which we did.

If I had kept the remodeling in pace with our budget we would not have ended up with a massive debt at the time the housing crash hit. We had added huge value to our home. But within months our area was one of the hardest hit in the housing crisis. The personal debt we owed brought enormous stress on top of the stress David already carried. I see now, this self-inflicted pain was another significant factor contributing to the failure in our marriage.

A year after we lost our church, we had to short sell our beautiful home. We lost everything we put into it and more.

Chapter 8

I Don't Have Enough

The ego is a fussy ol' geezer. It holds no peace. I know when my ego is speaking because I feel urgency or excitement. Do it before it's too late, says the ego. It's better to be right than happy, says the ego.

Hugh Prather

A second expression of our compulsive identity is the fear of not having enough of something we need to feel secure. We must acquire and accumulate more assets. And these assets come in a lot of surprising forms like:

Facts: I often need more information.
"I'm about to make an important decision. I'm anxious I might make a mistake. Until I research all the facts I won't feel settled."

Finances & possessions: Being financially secure is important to me.
"I just need a little more and I'll be okay. If I just had a nicer car or a larger home."

Friends: I need more friends.
"When it comes to friends, the more the merrier. I don't think I've ever met a stranger. I have a big contact list of people I like to hang out with. Having a lot of people in my life is key to my happiness."

Fun: I need more experiences.
"Getting away is just the best. Life can be so boring at home. I'm

bummed when I can't travel or have opportunities to do something different, get out and see the world."

Food: I can't get enough food.
"I get cranky if I'm served a small amount. Eating is one of my only pleasures. I sneak food. And I always go for seconds or thirds. Somehow it makes me feel better."

How many times a day do you think "I don't have enough of something I really need?" One guess where our fear of lack originates...

Then God said, "I give you every seed-bearing plant on the face of the whole earth and every tree that has fruit with seed in it. They will be yours for food." ..And it was so.
Gen 1:29

And the Lord God commanded the man, "You are free to eat from any tree in the garden; but you must not eat from the tree of the knowledge of good and evil, for when you eat from it you will certainly die."
Gen. 2:15

Now the serpent was more crafty than any of the wild animals the Lord God had made. He said to the woman, "Did God really say, 'you must not eat from any tree in the garden?'" The woman said to the serpent, "We may eat fruit from the trees in the garden, but God did say, 'You must not eat fruit from the tree that is in the middle of the garden...'"
Gen 3:1-2

The first couple goes from trusting in the generosity of their Father, to feeling the dread of scarcity. At the suggestion of the serpent they get the idea that between God and each other there might not be enough to satisfy and sustain them. They doubt. They get anxious. And eventually they give into the lie that God is withholding something they really need.

When our compulsive identity is driving scarcity, it can produce fear and anxiety in us. When it seems we don't have enough of something we feel we need, we can get tricked into thinking: "if I just get that one more thing, I'll be okay." And how long does that last? You know the drill. If you just get that promotion or a larger salary. And, when you get it, you use it to momentarily cover your fear. But soon the buzz wears off. You're strategizing your next move. You still need more.

As we look in on their story, it seems the first couple had everything they needed. But the temptation to reach for that one last thing that eluded them was too great. In the end their whole world collapsed.

When is enough, enough?

In the beginning, Adam and Eve go from believing their generous Dad has supplied everything they could ever need, to mistrusting his promise to provide for them. And they end up hiding in fear.

Are there some things you hide behind to feel safer? Is it more zeros in your bank account? Is it the number of friends you have? Or do you feel safer with more facts and information? There is nothing wrong with any of these things. But, when we need to acquire a never-ending amount of them to ease our fears, we are building on a constantly shifting, faulty foundation. And that seems even scarier.

Fig leaves for Adam and Eve were used to make insecurity go away. Those leaves are a metaphor to help us see how they were really masking the bigger issues of shame, fear and mistrust.

Fear says: "I don't have enough. God won't come through for me so I need to take matters into my own hands."

We often define ourselves by the assets we've accumulated. Or, we long for assets we feel we are somehow still missing.

In his book, *The Gift of Being Yourself*, David Benner has a great way of describing our problem. *"The false self is the tragic result of trying to steal something from God that we did not have to steal. Had we dared to trust God's goodness, we would have discovered that everything we could ever most deeply long for would be ours in God. Displacing God, we become a god unto our self. We become a false self."*

Our Compulsive Identity

Genesis 3:1-13, Luke 4:1-13

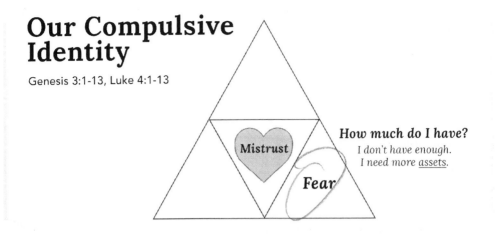

How much do I have?
I don't have enough.
I need more <u>assets</u>.

The Gospel of More Than Enough

Jesus, full of the Holy Spirit, returned from the Jordan and was led by the Spirit in the desert, where for forty days he was tempted by the devil. He ate nothing during those days, and at the end of them he was hungry. The devil said to him, "If you are the Son of God, tell this stone to become bread." Jesus answered, "It is written: 'Man does not live on bread alone.'"
Luke 4:1-4

Notice the tempter tries to make another identity challenge: "If you are..." He then questions Jesus ability to produce a simple loaf of bread...a very appealing scheme since Jesus had been in the desert 40 days without food. There never seems to be enough provision in the desert.

What's the temptation? Appetites. Fear of starvation. Lack. The tempter is provoking Jesus at the core of his identity to see if he can illicit any anxiety over a real human need.

It makes all the sense in the world that if Jesus had been alone in the desert, with no food, that he would be hungry, wondering where his next meal would be coming from. But, Jesus didn't believe he was alone and that there wasn't enough. His father had always been generous to him, and he was not going to stop providing now- even in harsh circumstances.

Many times, every day, we're all tempted by what we feel is our need for more. Jesus knew that because of the Father's love for him, he would be provided the things that matter most.

In his book, *Spiritual Notes to Myself*, author Hugh Prather says, "Our distress over money doesn't come so much from our lack of it as from our belief that it can protect us...you can feel safe, but only in God. As our place in God's heart dawns on us, we see money as one of the world's more amusing preoccupations..."

Fear comes when we leave this present moment and focus on future circumstances we can't even see. We're squandering a really good moment right now when we do this. But, even if this moment announces we are being evicted from our home- we are not lost. We are still very much alive and breathing, loved by God and a solution of some kind (though it may not be our solution or in our timing) is on the way.

Just like with approval, there is nothing wrong with funds, friends and facts. Where it goes screwy is when we subconsciously believe we can rid ourselves of fear by acquiring something to alleviate our fear.

Beefing up our internal security is what we need to shoot for, putting our trust in something / Someone that can never be taken away from us. In our hearts we believe this but how to actually do this eludes us constantly.

Over the last several years, we think we've come into an even clearer, more lasting way to stay connected to what we truly want and who we truly want to be. We'll share that in Step #3.

But, first here's how Jesus spoke to the issue.

Someone out of the crowd said, "Teacher, order my brother to give me a fair share of the family inheritance."

He replied, "Mister, what makes you think it's any of my business to be a judge or mediator for you?"

Speaking to the people, he went on, "Take care! Protect yourself against the least bit of greed. Life is not defined by what you have, even when you have a lot."

pg. 38

Then he told them this story: "The farm of a certain rich man produced a terrific crop. He talked to himself: 'What can I do? My barn isn't big enough for this harvest.' Then he said, 'Here's what I'll do: I'll tear down my barns and build bigger ones. Then I'll gather in all my grain and goods, and I'll say to myself, Self, you've done well! You've got it made and can now retire. Take it easy and have the time of your life!'

"Just then God showed up and said, 'Fool! Tonight you die. And your barn - full of goods - who gets it?'

"That's what happens when you fill your barn with Self and not with God."

"What I'm trying to do here is to get you to relax, not be so preoccupied with getting so you can respond to God's giving. People who don't know God and the way he works fuss over these things, but you know both God and how he works. Steep yourself in God-reality, God-initiative, God-provisions. You'll find all your everyday human concerns will be met. Don't be afraid of missing out. You're my dearest friends! The Father wants to give you the very kingdom itself.

"Be generous. Give to the poor. Get yourselves a bank that can't go bankrupt, a bank in heaven far from bank robbers, safe from embezzlers, a bank you can bank on. It's obvious, isn't it? The place where your treasure is, is the place you will most want to be, and end up being."
Luke 12:13-34 (The Message)

Inquiring Minds Want to Know

Reflect for a few minutes, as honestly as you can, about the possibility of your appetite for acquiring being a means of somehow covering a need to feel more safe in the world.

- Do you sometimes have the need to exhaust the possibilities when making a decision? Do you fear making a mistake due to insufficient details? Do you feel safer the more information you have about a person, business, event, plan, etc?

- Are you uncomfortable expressing emotions? Are you more comfortable with facts and data than with people?

- Do you sometimes feel unsafe? Do fear trusting God, other people or even yourself? Do you feel you need more support of some kind? See holes in every argument? Is the world a dangerous place? Do you feel unsafe to the point of super anxiety or feeling paranoid? Do you doubt and question everything and everyone? Are you afraid to spend money? Do you need a certain amount of money in the bank to feel secure?

- Do you sometimes fear depending on others because it probably won't turn out well? Are you sometimes afraid of being trapped in pain or deprivation? Is it hard to feel satisfied and content? Are you always looking for ways to maximize pleasure and side step emotional pain? Do you fear loss of freedom and fantasize about a better life? Can you distinguish between what you want and what you need?

In the next chapter we'll see the third "not enough" strategy of the compulsive identity that may be another contributing cause of your exhaustion.

Chapter 9

The Drive of Ambition

"Let's stop the glorification of busy."
Unknown

We break for lunch and the two of us drive to a local restaurant. We both want to get to the bottom of how this horrific failure could have happened to us and yet we're aware that the weight of our crisis is so heavy at the moment we have little energy to hear hard truth about ourselves or to make a ton of changes. Caron feels it's a lot to ask in light of the pain she's carrying. David is all-in but drained and dreading more shame-filled conversations around what's been discovered about him.

After lunch, we still have time to stretch our legs in the field behind the office where we're meeting. We walk off in different directions each seeking to find a few minutes of quiet wondering how this counseling intensive will be able to bridge the enormous gap of despair we feel over what has happened.

When everyone gathers back in the conference room Jim pulls out his folder and pen and Rich says, "We find it kind of interesting that both of you scored high as types who need to take the hill, get a lot accomplished. How does that resonate with you?

"Yeah." David says. "Being purposeful and productive has always been huge to me. For as long as I can remember, I've felt there was a special reason for my life. I thought God made me to do something good and I was determined to be out there, everyday getting it done in a big way. I got a lot of satisfaction from that.

But, there was always a nagging problem. My accomplishments never seemed big enough. They didn't match the vision in my head. I've been told all my life that I had so much potential. And, I felt guilty that I wasn't doing all I was fully capable of. I wanted to build one of the larger churches in the country. Some would say that's a worthy goal, right? The God-side of me always wanted to help as many people as possible find a loving relationship with him. And I was doing that. It was an authentic, driving passion in me and I wanted to see that same thing happen for many others. Eventually, our church grew to over 4,000. And what should have felt like joy at the accomplishment of a worthy goal, just made me want to crash and hide from people on my day off. I always felt the more success we had, the more everyone expected of me. The expectations never stopped.

"Hang on, Rich says, "you mean other people put expectations on you?"

"Well, yeah. I always felt that. I'd get great feedback on a series of messages so I knew I had to make the next series at least as good or better.

"In order to keep getting the same feedback?"

"Well, I didn't think of it that way. I felt God was calling our church to ever larger, more significant initiatives that would also require more resources and even sharper staff to carry them out. Even when I delegated stuff to others, which I had no problem doing most of the time, I'd usually have ten more things waiting for me to address.

The weight of meeting or exceeding our church budget never quit. I tried to keep a healthy perspective on the day in and day out, relentlessness of ministry. I took breaks in the middle of the day to walk outside and pray. And, most of the time, I had success resting in what I knew was God's grace for what He called me to do. But, there were times I failed miserably at responding to that."

"David, everyone has their limit," Rich says. There is only so much we can demand of our bodies, minds and souls. No matter what we believe, or have promised to those we love we all have our breaking point. Sounds like you expected yourself to live without limits, to be super human. You must have kept a crazy schedule."

"Actually," Caron breaks in, "people are usually surprised to hear that even though David left little room to breathe during working hours, he was home most nights of the week. He was a great hands-on dad. He was at nearly every game our boys ever played. We set aside a date night every week and we took vacations with and without our kids most every year. David is rare for his type in that he has no problem staying off his computer or turning off his cell phone at night. Strange as it may sound he is one of those people who can turn work off at night, at least, outwardly. He also journaled a lot to try to make sense of things. He memorized scripture to boost his dependence on God and he prayed daily about all he was carrying. He was not just a professional Christian. I often told people "I live with the man. Trust me; he's the real deal."

"Hmm, interesting." Rich says. "So, where do you think things broke down?"

"A couple of places," David says. I always felt like I had to keep it together for everyone. There never seemed to be a good time, or place for me to chill out and just be me where there were no expectations. Certainly, at home this was possible on most levels, but often, as Caron said, she'd want to talk about a pressing issue with her or the church. I always felt I needed to be there for her and boys.

"What else?"

"I always felt like I had to be 'on,' to be an example for everyone. Imagine a doctor who is never off call, even at the gym, around the neighborhood, at the mall or a restaurant, even getting his haircut-someone is always coming up and telling him about their ailments and he needs to bring healing on the spot. A lot of ministers feel like that. I know other people feel similar pressure with all their responsibilities, but you asked. A large church was great. I really loved my work. I loved what I saw happening in the lives of so many people. I felt tremendous fulfillment. I could not imagine a better vocation. But, it also meant I couldn't go anywhere in town without running into people from our church that needed my attention or concern, encouragement or prayer. At times it felt suffocating.

"Did people really put all that pressure on you? "

"Yeah, a lot of times."

"There was nothing in you that expected you to be superman? A selfless super human?"

"Well, probably.

"What about time for yourself?"

"I did take some time for myself. Sometimes, I went to a movie with one of my friends or if they had a boat we'd go out on the water. But most of my friends didn't have the same schedule I did. My Saturdays and Sundays were full. Several times a year I took international trips to train leaders. Being in a different place in the world was always refreshing and challenging for me in good ways. But, it rarely seemed to compensate very long for all the accumulated exhaustion.

And there were always fires to be put out. When the economy crash happened we had to lay off twenty-five really wonderful staff in order to meet our budget. I loved leading the staff but there was always a transition going on with someone and many of those required weeks or months of, sometimes, tense debates."

"How did you manage all the pressure?"

"I just sucked it up. That's what great leaders do. They just do what needs to be done. But, at least once every ten years or so, beginning in grad school, I found myself in the hospital with severe chest pains. Then after decades of all the people and crisis management, daily trouble shooting, strategic responsibilities, leadership coaching, study for messages and speaking Saturdays and Sundays I was near burn out."

"So what happened?"

"I think I started resenting things and believing lies."

"What kind of lies?"

"About the all weight I was carrying and the disappointments I felt around my failure to achieve all I knew I could do. I started believing the stress in our marriage might never change and the thought crept in that I deserved reprieves now and then for all my sacrifice across the board.

"I started thinking God was purposely holding me back or holding out on me. Maybe to keep me desperate for him or to keep me humble, I wasn't sure. Now I can't fathom the way my thinking got so twisted. Then, a woman began approaching me in the guise of friendship. And at first, I did not see it as anything other than genuine sisterly concern."

"Doesn't seem possible, does it, Caron?" Rich breaks in. "But, actually we see this happen a lot with guys like David. They can be totally clueless to someone else's agenda toward them because they are so focused on plowing through the work in front of them. It's like they have tunnel vision. They just can't see the whole field and what's going on in the periphery until it's too late."

"This is how clueless he was," Caron says. "The first time this woman mentions to him that she'd like to be better friends he came right home and told me about it. We both thought it was odd because we already knew this person. I sure made note of it, but David didn't think anything of it at the time."

"So, you didn't go looking for this," Rich says, "but someone "sensed" your neediness and eventually it felt good to have someone expressing concern about how hard you were working?"

"I was proud of how hard I worked. And around that time I was feeling like I rarely I got the appreciation I deserved for it. I'm embarrassed to say this now. I couldn't see it then but I was far too confident in my own moral strength to see this person's seduction. I actually prided myself, and many times told Caron and friends that this one area would never be an issue for me. Because I thought I was super strong there, I had nothing to worry about. What I didn't realize was that attitude of 'I've got this' left me totally unguarded."

With deep emotion David says, "That I could violate my marriage to Caron, devastated me beyond description. I hated myself. And I kept confessing my sin. To my dying day, this will be the single greatest regret of my life. Second is the loss of respect of our sons and their wives and the pain and dishonor I brought to our church and to Christ."

A long painful silence fills the room. Then Jim suggests we stop for a break. After about fifteen minutes or so we come back together and Jim says, "Caron, David is clear that he takes full responsibility for what he did. He also admitted he was overly confident in himself and was unaware of what was happening below the waterline of his soul. I'm going to ask a question that could be misunderstood as putting some sort of the blame on you. I am not suggesting that in any way. But I am curious as to the pressure you felt in your soul around the matter of achieving and what consequences that may have had on your own heart."

"I'm aware of always feeling like I had more abilities and gifts than I was using. I knew both of us had a lot of potential and that there was still so much more we hoped to do for the cause of Christ.

"When our boys were in high school I felt I needed to prove myself. Much of anything I'd accomplished had been attached to David and I wanted to see what I could do on my own. I authored several books and took speaking engagements at women's event and retreats. I got a sense of accomplishment in this but I'm aware it also added more burden on our family. I did these things on top of my work at the church. And I think how I handled the stress of those added opportunities contributed some to the reason we're here today.

"I like biographies, especially about spiritual leaders who have done great things at great sacrifice for the cause of Christ. I always believed I could and should be one of those people for God. When we married we both had this passion in common. It's not a cliché that I was so grateful for all God had done I wanted to give back so that others could experience what I had. I know I held a high standard for what this should look like for me, for us, for our family and our church."

"So do you think this high standard ever went too far?"

"Until all this happened I don't think I would have been able to recognize it. But, yes, now I believe it did. It devastates me that, I, in any way contributed to the vulnerability of our marriage. I have a streak of perfectionism. It definitely pushes me to do more, to work hard and go big with excellence. People are usually happy with the outcome of things I'm involved with but what I go through and what I put others through to get there has often not been pretty."

"Anything else?"

"Well, especially in earlier years, if a family left our church it would sink me. I'd worry that something was wrong with us or that we weren't doing enough of the right things to keep people. People leave churches for all kinds of reasons but somehow I felt they were personally abandoning me. My depression over these incidents affected David, though he tried not to show it. My anxiousness over the successes and failures of our church just multiplied his pressure and stress. At times I know I was not the peaceful safe haven he really needed.

"I'm now coming to realize, not all, but some part of my genuine passion for the cause of Christ through our church came from my own need to feel okay."

"Well guys," Rich says. "You've certainly accomplished a lot, you've carried a lot on your shoulders, and now you've collapsed from the weight of it. First, I want to say, it's easy for any of us to mix up our own need to feel okay about ourselves with our genuine passion to expand the cause of Christ. We are all a mixture of motives in everything we do. But, for the future, one of the little known tricks to determining if we're working from guilt or love is how much striving, anxiety or conflict is going on in us or through us as we do it. The Spirit doesn't need life to be perfect, or to appear successful or ambitious because He does all things from the stance of Perfect Love.

We are deeply sorry for the pain you and everyone else in your life is going through. It's going to take time before you can see your way to a new normal. But, we can promise you, from our own stories and from others we've counseled, if you do the work we suggest - your new normal can turn out to be even better than your best days before. God has given you severe mercy in this catastrophe. It'll be tough, but totally worth it. You will see."

Chapter 10

I Can't Do Enough

If I had a message to my contemporaries it is surely this: Be anything you like, be madmen, drunks, and bastards of every shape and form, but at all costs avoid one thing: success... If you are too obsessed with success, you will forget to live. If you have learned only how to be a success, your life has probably been wasted.

Thomas Merton

Does some part of our struggle for achievement resonate with you? Is there something you've needed to prove? Or is there someone you've needed to prove wrong? Was there someone who did not believe you could accomplish something, so now you'll show them? What story have you believed that fuels your need for accomplishment? And how is that going for you? Your family? Your work associates?

The third expression of our compulsive identity creates stress in our daily life through our relentless striving for more and more accomplishment.

We all want to do 'the right thing.' None of us wakes up in the morning thinking: "I'd just like to go out there and do something stupid."

When Adam and Eve did the wrong thing, which is fascinating, because they were actually trying to do a right thing... They had wanted to become like God. But by believing the exaggerated truth that the tempter offers them, it ends up being a horrible thing. Then God appears…

And (God) said, "Who told you that you were naked? Have you eaten from the tree that I commanded you not to eat from?" The man said, "The woman you put here with me—she gave me some fruit from the tree, and I ate it." Then the Lord God said to the woman, "What is this you have done?" The woman said, "The serpent deceived me, and I ate."
Genesis 3:11-13

So, they start blaming each other. And blame often comes from a place of guilt. Whenever we do the wrong thing, or we don't feel like we've done enough of the right thing, we feel guilty.

Sometimes, we feel guilty for not being there for our parents, or for a sick friend or our kids, if we travel or have been distracted too often by our own issues. We may feel regret that we're letting someone down.

Something we have personally experienced and we hear all the time is someone feeling like they haven't lived up to their full potential. "Well, how do we know this? Who establishes the mark we need to reach? Who actually knows our full potential and what we've been designed to do and be in this world? It's a funny thing, "potential -" when we reach what was the last notch of our fullest potential, the mark mysteriously moves and we must reach for a whole new level. And something pushes us to do this again and again.

Apparently, this is part of football coach, Urban Meyers, story as well.

In a recent article in the Orlando Sentinel, Wayne Coffey*, co-author of Above the Line: Lessons in Leadership and Life from a Championship Season said, *"Urban said if he didn't leave UF (University of Florida) when he did and the changes he had to make in his life he doesn't think he would even be alive today. He told me the story about the night they won their second national championship and were having a big celebration. In the middle of the party, the coaches noticed that Urban wasn't at the party. An assistant coach went over to Meyer's office and found him there, with his door closed, working on recruiting for the next year. The assistant asked: 'What in the heck are you doing? We just won the national championship?' Urban was so driven and his perspective was so warped that he was sure if he even took a few minutes to celebrate his amazing achievement, he would fall behind."*
pg. 50

Soon after this Meyer resigned as head coach at University of Florida citing the need to attend to his health and family.

We get this. We've both felt the tug of that imaginary stat sheet in the sky that would show we had done enough. In David's case he felt "people" expected more from him. So, he kept trying to get more impressive things done. Things he thought were good, "that God called him to do." From both our stories we've come to realize the majority of the stress we carry is completely of our own making.

Perfectionism is one huge driver for some of us facing the draw of ambition. Dr. Brene Brown says perfectionism is "a way of thinking and feeling that says if I look perfect, do it perfect, work perfect, and live perfect I can avoid or minimize shame, blame and judgment."

For perfectionists it's often go big or go home. They struggle with black and white thinking and do things in extremes. Life is an all or nothing game and once a goal is set nothing can stop them from accomplishing it. Being average or mediocre is something perfectionists strive hard against so it's no surprise that perfectionists are also associated with workaholics. Even though a perfectionist acknowledges his standards are relentlessly high (think Steve Jobs) and somewhat unreasonable they believe the levels of excellence and productivity more than make up for any unpleasantness to themselves or others along the way.

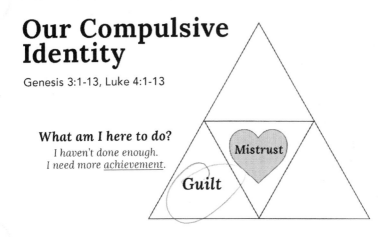

Our Compulsive Identity

Genesis 3:1-13, Luke 4:1-13

What am I here to do?
I haven't done enough.
I need more underachievement.

Mistrust

Guilt

Did Jesus do enough?

Back in the desert at the temptation of Jesus...

> "The devil led (Jesus) up to a high place and showed him in an instant all the kingdoms of the world. And he said to him, "I will give you all their authority and splendor, for it has been given to me, and I can give it to anyone I want to. So if you worship me, it will all be yours." Jesus answered, "It is written: 'Worship the Lord your God and serve him only.'"
> **Luke 4: 5-8**

The tempter says to Jesus - "I can give you all authority." Notice Jesus doesn't argue with him. He knew Adam and Eve's original role of Kingdom authority had already been handed over to the enemy so Jesus knew the enemy had authority to give. And Jesus also knew that if he did it the tempter's way he would be representing enemy initiatives and not his Father in heaven.

Jesus' response was that he would only worship His Father and achieve what His Father gifted and directed him to do.

Jesus didn't need the identity boost the tempter came offering because he knew he already possessed everything he would ever need for the life he lived. He knew greater was the One in him than the one who was in the world. And even though Jesus does endure death he still ends up getting all the power and authority the enemy tried to tempt him with (John 13:3).

Jesus was ambitious and got humanly tired from a days work. But he didn't try to heal everyone everywhere he went. There was probably still a little left for him to do at the time of his earthly departure. He could have reached more people, had a greater impact if he had just tried harder, had more meetings, and met the right people. We have every reason to believe the kingdom of God would have expanded faster had he been even more creative with his time and effort. Yet, even at age thirty three he had the presence of heart to say as his martyrdom approached, "I have brought you glory on earth by finishing the work you gave me to do" (John 17:4).

Jesus lived and worked out of a perpetual connection with and assurance of his sonship to God his Father. He was so secure in that relationship that there was nothing for him to prove to himself or to anyone else. When you already have the approval of the King of Heaven what more can the world offer you?

We realize now, that a good bit of the good work we have done was mixed with the work our compulsive identities piled on us to accomplish in order to cover self–imposed guilt.

What's your story?

Take a minute now and sit with these questions as you think about your own need to achieve:

- What "story" are you living into? Is there a narrative underneath your accomplishments that pushes you to do more and more and more? What is it? Where did it come from?

- Whose voice do you hear saying you will be super amazing or sadly disappointing?

- What are you afraid you will miss out on if you don't accomplish more things?

- What words are you listening to hear about your achievements from someone important?

- Is some of your work about trying to pay someone back, maybe even God, for the life you've been given---even though you know there will never be enough payback?

- Do you have the need to feel powerful, not vulnerable, and do your accomplishments give you a sense of power?

- Are you a forceful person who must be listened to because you know the right way to get things done?

- Are you a fighter? Is it your way or the highway?

- Do you mainly feel secure when you're in control?

- Do people say you're always pushing? Against things, circumstances, other people?

- Is "weakness" a bad word to you?

- Is independence a big value for you?

- Are people out to take advantage of you?

Or....

- Do you procrastinate beginning a task if it can't be done perfectly?

- Do you strive to produce as a reaction to being told you are lazy?

- Do you think others won't notice you unless you exert yourself in a big way?

- Do you think the world is not "right" and it needs someone like you to help fix it?

- Do you have very high standards that few others can meet, not even yourself?

- Are you often motived to get things done because of anger that things are not being done right out there?

Note : Wayne Coffey : *Urban would not have survived.* Orlando Sentinel pg.,1, Nov 14, 2015

Our Compulsive Identity

Genesis 3:1-13, Luke 4:1-13

Who am I?
I'm not enough.
I need more <u>approval</u>.

What am I here to do?
I haven't done enough.
I need more <u>achievement</u>.

How much do I have?
I don't have enough.
I need more <u>assets</u>.

Chapter 11

Your Default Position

Self-deception occurs automatically. This is part of what psychologists mean when they say that our defense mechanisms operate in the unconscious. It is also part of what the theologians mean when they speak of original sin. We don't have to choose self-deception. It is our default option.

David Benner

The battlefield for our character isn't just around surface behavior or moralistic sins. If we stay focused on those, we'll miss what's actually driving us beneath the surface.

At some point, our compulsive identity breaks down, fails us, gets exposed, or, at least, gets a big bucket of ice water thrown in its face. We need a wake up call to fully see what it has been up to. Whatever served us earlier to find some level of satisfaction, security, and significance suddenly no longer works. And when that happens we either double down on our efforts or we begin to let go and surrender.

After many decades of intense ministry and family life, David began to believe a subtle series of lies about God, himself and several others. A potent combination of his compulsive identity and the slick devices of the enemy generated those lies. The consequences of those beliefs cracked him wide open. And before it was over, the pain and public humiliation he endured was so severe, several times, he had thoughts of taking his life.

In time, God has given us both grace to face the trauma of our situation and to learn the lessons it brought to us. From the most impossible circumstances has come the true and deeply satisfying life we always suspected was possible but, in part, remained out of reach.

There is nothing wrong with achievement. There is nothing wrong with ambition. There is nothing wrong with gaining or gathering assets. But when their use gets exaggerated in us, when we become overly attached to our roles or status, we never seem to get enough of them.

The enemy of your life has three strategies: Shame, Fear, and Guilt. These are the roots of our suffering and anxiety, of our train wrecks and even, perhaps, some of our successes.

Throughout your life you deal with each of these strategies. But we believe one of them is your "home base,' your internal default position. One of them keeps returning to plague and pester you. It drives you to do and say things that do not reflect your true self in God.

3 Root Questions
in Search of Our Identity

Who am I?
Compulsive Answer: "I'm not enough" **(Shame)**

How much do I have?
Compulsive Answer: "I don't have enough" **(Fear)**

What am I here to do?
Compulsive Answer: "I haven't done enough" **(Guilt)**

Shame. Fear. Or Guilt.
Do you know which one is your home base?

The enemy tries to get us to buy in to these strategies through temptations of approval, assets, and achievement. All the stories of the Bible can be seen through these strategies. And all the stories of human history are there as well. They play out everyday in individuals, families, organizations, churches, companies, and even nations.

The Apostle Paul said: *Put on the full armor of God, so that you can take your stand against the devil's schemes* (Ephesians 6:1). These tricks are certainly nothing new. But, they sure as heck are effective.

We fall for them anytime we trust our own views of reality and seek our own ways to control it. A healthier play is when we're fully grounded in and trust God's view of our reality and live convinced of his utmost concern for our well fare.

We love this statement by Anthony DeMillo: *"If you made a list of everything you own, everything you think of as you, everything that you prefer, that list would be the distance between you and the living truth."*

Step #2

Plant Yourself in the Source of Your True Identity

Learning how to recognize and live out of the truest part of ourselves, that part which cannot be improved on, expanded or reduced, made in the image of God, is the most significant and most challenging of all human achievements.

There are a number of interchangeable nametags for our true identity: our created self, our true self, our eternal or God-self, our spirit, or new creation in Christ.

Chapter 12

The True You

We must stumble and fall. And that does not mean reading about falling. We must actually be out of the drivers seat for while, or we will never learn how to give up control to the Real Guide.

Richard Rohr

We wish it were not so but, it seems, for many of us, it isn't until we come to the end of ourselves, get knocked flat off our horse, that we start to see there is actually, a higher, more satisfying and more peace-filled way to live.

Our view of this epiphany is laid out in the three steps of this book. This is our journey to breakthrough and we believe it can help create lasting transformation for you too; where there is nothing more for you to prove, where you start fully experiencing the life you were born to live.

In Step One we pinpoint what drives our conditioned/false identity. Here we become aware of how our habitual thoughts about our self and our reactivity are truly affecting our lives and relationships. We begin to see the suffering our negative, untrue beliefs produce for us and for others. We recognize we are living much of the time in illusion. We start to notice our repetitive cycles of proving, protecting and promoting and the stress they produce in others and in us.

Now in Step Two we plant ourselves at the Source of our true identity. We start to experience the beginnings of what it means to be a perfect spiritual being having an imperfect human experience. Whether it comes by deep grace or difficult circumstances the veil is being torn away and we begin to desire to live into a more meaning-filled life. This doesn't happen overnight, nor does it mean we close up shop and run off to a monastery, (even though that might not be a bad idea every once in awhile.) Our desires and choices draw more and more on the transcendent even though we are still very much alive and well in our transient world. Here we see the reality that God is the Ultimate Source of our true identity. Our eyes are opened just in time.

Whatever brings us here, it has probably been a breaking open of some kind, and it's brought considerable pain and disorientation. Everything that worked before no longer makes sense. People we counted on before are gone or no longer available. On some level, the person we thought we were, no longer exists. And we are finally open to something new. We need a new paradigm, something that can endure any drama or difficulty we will ever encounter again.

So, what exactly is the truth about who you are; what you have; or what you could be doing? Well, one of the things that grab our attention regularly is that our God-self identity is pure gift.

David Benner talks about it this way: *"We speak of certain people as being self made, but no one is truly their own creation. Personhood is not an accomplishment; it is a gift. Our true self, the self we're becoming in God is something we receive from God. Any other identity is of our own making and is an illusion."*

Trusting your created identity is embracing God's view of your reality and that; regardless of what's going on He is lovingly holding you in that reality. Your created identity is eager to trust more in what God sees and thinks about you and everything else in your world. When you can do this it leads smack into the satisfaction, security, and significance you've been looking for. This is you in pure freedom, with nothing to prove. WOW!

When you trust your compulsive identity you are banking on your own view of reality being accurate and on you being able to control that reality. It trusts in what you see, what you think about yourself, God, and the rest of the world. When you live from this identity, the proving and accumulating and ambition never end. UGH!

In the search for our true identity we all seem to have at least three root questions:

---

3 Root Questions in Search of Our Identity

Who am I?

How much do I have?

What am I here to do?

In previous chapters we looked at how our compulsive identity tries to answer those questions. Now let's look at how our true identity speaks to them. It's a startling contrast!

Chapter 13

Lavishly Loved

God speaks to us in a thousand voices each with the same clear message: I love you. Please trust me on this one.

Hugh Prather

The first expression of our true identity is that we are irrevocably and lavishly loved as we are.

Now, before you say, "Yeah, yeah, I know God loves me. Tell me something I don't know." Let us just say, we'd heard that before too, and we'd taught it and believed it to our depths. And, we still ended up with a train wreck. So, for us, as fully convinced as we were of God's love, something got lost in translation. We have a suspicion this might be your story, too, at least, part of the time. So, hang with us on this.

Before I formed you in the womb I knew you, before you were born I set you apart...
Jeremiah 1:5

This is a great mystery: even before you were born you were already joined to God, found in God and lavishly loved by God. This continues to be true for you right now. Regardless of what has happened. Not one atom of God's love for you has been depleted. And you need never beg for more love again—all you'll ever need is constantly being supplied.

Back in the beginning we see this:

Then God said, 'Let us make mankind in our image, in our likeness...'

So God created mankind in his own image, in the image of God he created them; male and female he created them. God blessed them and said to them..."
Genesis 1:26-28

The FIRST thing God does at human creation is to establish them in their identity. God blesses them. They have done absolutely nothing. They've accomplished nothing; have not attempted to live exemplary lives. They haven't been kind or generous or obedient to their Father God. Still, the first thing he does is grant them his favor.

Recently, an extra precious baby, Judah, was added to our family. This kid has it made. He is cared for from sun up to sundown and into the wee hours of every morning. He is cradled and kissed and adored and fed and diapered and kissed and adored some more. Then when his grandparents come over there is more cuddling and cooing, kissing and adoring. The child is constantly bathed in a sea of love.

Would that every child in the world had Judah's love advantage. Oh, wait. In the truest reality, the most reliable spiritual sense of things, every child, student and adult actually does have that advantage.

Therefore, as dearly loved children... walk in the way of love...
Ephesians 5:1

Each of us, have received the unending love of our Heavenly Father whether we know it or feel it or not. Our problem seems to be that we don't always know how to access that love. We fail to experience the profound love of God where it can actually do us the most good. We'll talk more on how to do this in Step #3.

The Gift that Truly Keeps Giving

At creation God's love is eternally installed in you. It's pure gift. Sounds a lot like grace, which we might argue, are one in the same. Your life was a gift and God's love is sheer grace. And this is true for you in all seasons. Whether your life is up and to the right or crashed in a heap.

All God does is bless. Blessing is the family business. Notice Adam and

Eve didn't begin in original sin. They began in original blessing branded forever with God's love and image inside them. Those who believe we all start out as screw-ups couldn't be more wrong. You began as someone participating in the most positive action in history, and the rest of your life you are invited to live from that truth.

In Genesis 1:26, God says this *"Let us make man in our image."* So, let's pause for a moment. What's up with that word "us"?

The first four words of the Bible are "In the beginning, God…" (Genesis 1:1). The Hebrew word for God here is "Eloheim." The suffix of this word "im" is plural. It's the difference between saying, "I have a car" versus "I have cars."

From the get-go there is a singular Divine Being organized in plurality. At our origin…"in the image of God" we are birthed from the heart of the family/trinity of God, a Three in One community of divine reciprocating love. So, the scripture could read, let us make man stamped with our communal image of unending love…

> *We love because he first loved us.*
> **1 John 4:19**

Before your parents ever even noticed each other, you were already loved and known by God. You were deeply valued in God's heart. The One who loved you before time birthed you into time. The Father, Son, and Spirit got great pleasure from anticipating the day they would put you on display for the world to see.

Divine love can be nothing less than perfect. And that perfect love that has been lavishly, abundantly filling you has been spoken over your life and is fully installed and activated in you right now.

Whenever we seek a counterfeit way or look for love and adoration outside this Divine space within us, it will fail us. Yet, we keep hoping and acting as if this this isn't true. We keep knocking, sometimes pounding on all those "other doors" until finally that one huge door we were counting on finally falls open …only to reveal a disappointing lack of substance behind it after all.

Knowledge or Transformation

It's not enough to know about God's love. Most of the folks we've associated with over the years know something about God's love. They've studied it. Most can quote multiple scriptures to confirm this truth. It's not enough to hear about God's love. You've probably heard countless talks on it.

And even though our churches are full of worship proclaiming the glory of God's infinite love, we still struggle to experience it.

Staying grounded at our core to the truth that we are fixed for life in Deepest Love is something we often remind ourselves of. It easily evaporates with all the competing influences of our lives. Maybe that's why Jesus spends all of John 15 emphasizing abiding in him and his love. It's significant that one of the last things he asks of his disciples is to *"Remain in my love"* (John 15:9).

You can think about the love of your spouse or child or friend and it's a nice comforting thought. But, it doesn't impact you at the same level as the warmth of their actual presence or the joy in conversation around a meal. We would never settle for just thinking great thoughts about our loved ones if we had a choice. Yet, that's what we do in our relationship with God. God is nearer and greater than our limited thoughts about him. And he invites us to actually experience him daily so we can anchor ourselves in him.

So how can we know if God's love is transforming us and becoming the source of our true identity? One indicator might be in the way we reply to the question *"Who are you?"*.

If our predominate thought is:
- "I am a school teacher"
- "I am the parent of three kids"
- "I'm the CEO of a company"
- "I'm divorced"
- "I'm bankrupt"
- "I'm a failure"

We still may be in the habit of seeing our true ourselves as the roles we play. When we over identify with our roles or relationships we tend to lose sight of what's ultimately true about us and on some level we might still be locked into believing that we are the form or container we present to the world. But those roles are our shells, not our substance.

A part of David's story is that he totally believed in the love of God. He had been taught it from childhood, had memorized scriptures on it, had spoken messages about it. He created sayings around it. And, he had personally experienced God's love in many ways over his lifetime. He thought this was as good as it gets.

What he did not know was how to consistently access God's love at a deep enough place to transform his view of himself.

If you had asked David - "Who are you, really?" He probably would have given a list of his roles and responsibilities: a husband, father, leader, pastor, friend, etc. His first thought would not have been, "I'm an ordinary guy who is grounded at the core of my being in God's unending love - and it's more than enough."

See what great love the Father has lavished on us, that we should be called children of God! And that is what we are!
1 John 3:1

The word "lavished" here speaks of the overwhelming, abundance of a cascading waterfall of God's value, desire, and love for you. He felt this way when you were conceived. He will feel this way when you meet him in the end. So, why would God think anything else about you between those times?

The book of Psalms says, "His love endures forever." Every other love, accolade, accomplishment, compliment, asset, or promotion is fleeting and flawed. Only God's love - that permeates and grounds you - will endure through all your experiences and keep you till the end.

Our True Identity

Genesis 1:26-31, Luke 3:21-22

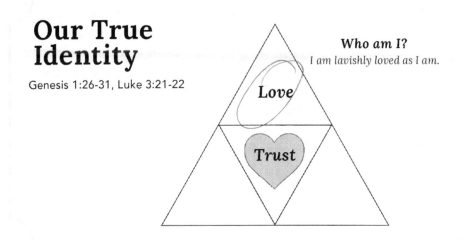

Love

Trust

What Does it Take to Please God?

When the scene opens on the ministry of Jesus the first thing God does is to establish Jesus' identity, just like He did with Adam and Eve, before they began their public lives.

At that time Jesus came from Nazareth in Galilee and was baptized by John in the Jordan. Just as Jesus was coming up out of the water, he saw heaven being torn open and the Spirit descending on him like a dove and a voice came from heaven: "You are my Son, whom I love; with you I am well pleased" (Mark 1:9-11).

"This is my son…" Through the voice of God, Jesus' value and credibility is instantly established. Before Jesus speaks his first killer parable, or does one miracle or performs even the smallest thing "pleasing to God" he learns God is already pleased with him. There will be nothing for him to prove. The God of the Universe already fully approves of who he is.

Jesus' whole orientation to who he was had everything to do with whose He was. His orientation was not himself, or his power, or his wisdom or his goodness. His orientation was from Someone who would never change.

Jesus' earthly life was going to take on multiple forms: baby; child; teenager; adult; adored; hated; wanted; un-wanted; popular; un-popular; full; hungry; successful; and failure. But who Jesus really was, was not found in any of those forms. They were just his experiences. And they were all temporary, like vapor.

Your life will go through many changing forms: child; teenager; adult; adored; hated; wanted; un-wanted; popular; un-popular; full; hungry; successful; and failure. But you are not any of those forms. You've experienced them but they are not you. Who you are is one who is lavishly and eternally loved by God, everything else - all other forms, may seem to some like a big deal but in light of things eternal they are a puff of smoke.

We all hunger for:

- a center...
- a compass..
- an orientation...
- a north star...

that never changes.

God says to you "*You are my son (my daughter), whom I love, in whom I am well pleased*". And whatever God said of Jesus is also something we can claim for ourselves.

> *Praise be to the God and Father of our Lord Jesus Christ, who has blessed us in the heavenly realms with every spiritual blessing in Christ.* **Ephesians 1:3**

The Most Secure Root

To ultimately thrive with the joy and satisfaction you've been hungering for, you must be rooted in something foundationally larger than the passing forms of this life. You must be dipped in the depths of Someone greater than your self.

If we've never had anyone believe in us, affirm us, or delight in us, we may be lacking a secure foundation. And when that happens we can end up spending our whole lives trying to convince ourselves (or get others to affirm) "I'm really ok. In fact, I'm wonderful. Hey, can't you see how great I am?"

But, we don't fully believe it.

That significant blessing, that Word of Grace, that Source of our confidence in this world must come from Someone Greater than ourselves. That's one of the primary roles of fathers and mothers. In them we learn to know who we are. From them we learn if we are conditionally or unconditionally loved. The best ones get us pointed in the right direction but even this will not prove to be enough to carry us through all situations our entire lives.

That's when we look to our culture to affirm who we are. But our culture can't ever assure us we're okay because the mark of what's good, valuable and worthy is constantly shifting. We know if we're ever going to feel approved by our culture we've got to keep changing to meet its demands. Eventually, we burn out just trying to keep up.

Or we latch on to a boyfriend, girlfriend, spouse or child to find approval, to hear who we are and how valuable we are to them. But, even this relationship is suspect because those who profess the highest devotion can at some point fail us and before it's all over one of us will die.

Is there anyone stable enough, constant enough, unchanging enough, faithful enough, powerful enough to hold us safely and securely at the core of our identity through whatever may come?

We need Someone who can endure with us through all the heat and tests, disappointments and defeats of our lives. We need a way to defeat our internal shame.

Jesus found the way to do this through the voice-affirming blessing of his Father. "This is my beloved son in whom I love and in whom I am well pleased. " Once Jesus hears this you can't stop him. He's now fully anchored in his own true identity and his own soul. His irrevocable sonship becomes his permanent orientation. It gets him through hell and back.

And it can do that for you, too.

Knowing God loves you, regardless, gives you full freedom to love and accept every part of yourself, even the crappy parts. Until you know yourself and see yourself immersed in your true self in God your real life has not yet begun. If you continue to live under the illusion that who you are is a 'form' - as in, "I'm a doctor, teacher, wealthy person, etc." you will constantly be dodging and shifting, unstable and insecure about your place in the world. Your status will constantly change and your life will eventually feel anchorless.

Once you truly begin to experience your continuous connection to God's lavish love, nothing can stop you. Nothing and no one can take away from you what is given to you by God. Every gift God gives is irrevocable (Romans 11:29).

> *Keep yourselves in God's love as you wait for the mercy of our Lord Jesus Christ to bring you to eternal life.*
> **Jude 1:21**

Chapter 14

Sufficient Supply

From moment to moment, I remember with surprise that I am satisfied, even though everything is not yet fulfilled. I lack nothing. (God) satisfies me in all things. To know and taste the secret good that is present but is not known to those who, because they are restless and because they are discontent and because they complain, cannot apprehend it.

Thomas Merton

We spend some part of everyday now trying to be more aware of comments, anxieties, actions and reactions that rise in us automatically and drive a lot of our unconscious behavior. Our goal is to catch negative thoughts in the act because 1) they are usually untrue 2) they cause us untold suffering 3) we want to truly enjoy the life God designed us to live.

One of the habitual thinking patterns that plague many of us is fear. Yes, some fear is healthy, as in the case of self protection, but we're talking about borderline to unhealthy fear of anything we don't understand, can't control and, for the purposes of this book, the fear of lack that comes from thinking we don't have enough of something we need right now or will need in the future.

You have a number of very human, legitimate needs. And what is most true about you is that God knows those needs and has already been supplying them. One of the things we want to do in this chapter is help open your eyes to all the significant assets you already possess. We want to show you what is really already yours in your own moment-by-moment experience.

In the Beginning... There was Abundance

One of the first things God does in creation is show the first couple how well they are set for groceries. It's like God knows fear of lack will be an issue so he makes a point to speak to it before the question "where's the beef?" gets asked.

> "I give you every seed-bearing plant on the face of the whole earth and every tree that has fruit with seed in it. They will be yours for food. 30 And to all the beasts of the earth and all the birds in the sky and all the creatures that move along the ground—everything that has the breath of life in it—I give every green plant for food."
> **Genesis 1:29-30**

A simple paraphrase of this might be: "all these plants are here to provide you a reproducible and (at that time eternal) provision of food. I don't want you to worry about a thing."

Our needs are not wrong, or carnal; or less than spiritual. Human beings have a boatload of God-given legitimate needs. What gets us in trouble is when we fear our needs –whatever they are – are not going to be met and we start frantically looking around for option B.

> (God)... has given us everything we need pertaining to life...
> **2 Peter 1:3**

This is a good place to stop and try to name some of the things you're missing and really need right now. What are they?

_____

_____

_____

Upon Further Review

If you look closer, and pare your "needs" down to what you actually need to be alive and well…. you probably have all you need right now.

If you're reading this book chances are you aren't starving to death, you're clothed, even if you don't own it, you probably have shelter or, at minimum, access to shelter today; and you've got unique abilities and potential opportunities.

Our compulsive minds prod us with: "Yes, that's true, but, what about next week? I'm not sure I've got enough … or what about next year… or when I retire?" Truthfully, we don't really know what we're going to need at any date in the future. We have the illusion we know what we'll need. But, when we get there, if we get there, God promises a fresh supply of assets sufficient enough for whatever situation we find ourselves in. We have no promise for our future except that God will be there with us and we know from taking stock of our present experience with him that when that time comes we will be okay.

As we write this book our own trust in God's sufficiency is being tested. As you read earlier several years ago we both lost our jobs at the church. For a while we made it on severance then we braced ourselves for all that would come next. Along with our income we lost our home and retirement benefits. And for the last several years we have lived very much by faith as we sense God's leading to proceed in the direction of a local and virtual teaching, coaching and consulting ministry. We can assure you, at this writing, we feel the acute tension of "Is this going to work long term? Are we going to make it?" Yet, by all indications so far we are being held and gently cared for day-by-day, week-by-week.

One example of being invisibly cared for came several months ago when we needed technical help launching *The Live True Podcast*. David was totally stuck. We had already asked technical favors from those we knew and we couldn't move forward without figuring out a certain code issue. So, David went to Facebook in hopes someone there might know where to point him. Within a few minutes our friend, Ami, who lives in Michigan, offered the exact solution we needed.

At that point, Ami, who owns Uplevel Creative Agency, was facing economic issues of her own but she quickly and graciously helped us out. Now Ami has another small stream of income from assisting us each week and we are getting the technical help we need to create life-changing tools like this book.

But, before you go frantically looking "out there" to get your needs met, let's see what you actually have going for you right now. And, let's start with your body.

Your Invisible Support

Buckle your seat belt.

Your body is made up of billions and billions of atoms. And all these atoms have been crafted together to create your unique DNA unlike anyone else who has ever lived.

Scientists tell us that, every so many minutes, hundreds of millions of your atoms will die and leave your body and, at the same instant, hundreds of millions of replacement atoms are supplied back to you. (Maybe this explains why you may be feeling a little weird today.) Seriously, when all these new atoms enter your body they blend back into exactly who you are--- so you don't end up looking like your next-door neighbor.

At this very moment, without any effort from you, you are breathing. Actually, you are being breathed. You are being supplied all the oxygen you need and it's being delivered to every part of your body free of charge. It's estimated that over the course of a day, you average somewhere between 17,000-30,000 breaths!

Your heart pumps about 2000 gallons of blood through its chambers every day. And it beats more than 100,000 times in twenty-four hours to achieve this feat.

Thousands of times a day your body tries to prevent you from getting cancer. Cancer is formed when cells are altered in a way that re-programs their DNA, and it's estimated that tens of thousands of cells suffer cancer-causing lesions every day. But your body sends special enzymes scampering to search DNA strands for faults and then it fixes them before they become tumors.

There are approximately 50,000 thoughts that pass through your mind each day. If you do the math, that is 41 thoughts every minute.

You shed more than 1 million skin cells every single day but they are replenished automatically, to save you from turning transparent and becoming exposed. Your skin is actually an organ and the largest one you have.

Your liver is so busy over the course of a day, that it's nearly impossible to summarize its activities. It manufactures cholesterol, vitamin D and blood plasma; it identifies the nutrients your body needs and stores some away for future use; it filters 1.5 quarts of blood every minute and produces 1 quart of bile every day to help you break down your food. Your liver is an entire health factory continuously running inside of you.

Each of your kidneys contains 1 million tiny filters that work together to filter an average of 2.2 pints of blood every minute- that's 3,168 pints or 46 gallons every single day, despite each kidney only being the size of a fist. If that wasn't enough, they also expel an average of 2.5 pints of toxic urine from your body each day.

And most amazing of all, your body cells are regenerating themselves every single day without any prompting. This means you have an entirely new set of taste buds every ten days, new nails every 6-10 months, new bones supporting you every ten years and even a new heart every 20 years.

Speaking of support, your neck and shoulders are supporting your head. Your bones, muscles and your chest cavity are supporting your breathing. Without them you would collapse immediately. And, while we're at it, the furniture supporting you right now was made by someone who is helping to support you whether they know it or not. The furniture holding you is being supported by something called 'Earth' that is supporting all of us. And there are enormous planets and stars that hold our planet in orbit.

All of this, and much, much, more goes on every moment of everyday as a free and generous gift to you, no thanks required. And this is just a tiny representation of God's provision for you.

Our True Identity

Genesis 1:26-31, Luke 3:21-22

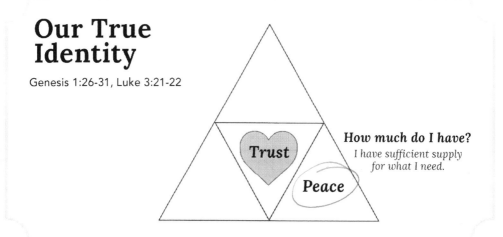

How much do I have?
I have sufficient supply for what I need.

Trust

Peace

Plenty of Good News

At that time Jesus came from Nazareth in Galilee and was baptized by John in the Jordan. Just as Jesus was coming up out of the water, he saw heaven being torn open and the Spirit descending on him like a dove and a voice came from heaven *"You are my Son, whom I love..."* (Mark 1:9-11).

What does love do? Love gives. It's the nature of love. This is symbolized for Jesus the Human One (or Son of Man) in the descending of the Holy Spirit on him. He gets 'filled.'

Jesus has plenty of needs as he begins his earthly ministry and they intensify over the next several years. But, this encounter with God's spirit demonstrates to him that no matter what his need is, one way or another, he will be taken care of through the love of his Father. And, what is true for Jesus is true for us.

Listen to how Jesus perfectly reflects his trust in God's care for him.

> *"If you decide for God, living a life of God-worship, it follows that you don't fuss about what's on the table at mealtimes or whether the clothes in your closet are in fashion. There is far more to your life than the food you put in your stomach, more to your outer appearance than the clothes you hang on your body. Look at the birds, free and unfettered, not tied down to a job description, careless in the care of God. And you count far more to him than birds.*

"Has anyone by fussing in front of the mirror ever gotten taller by so much as an inch? All this time and money wasted on fashion—do you think it makes that much difference? Instead of looking at the fashions, walk out into the fields and look at the wildflowers. They never primp or shop, but have you ever seen color and design quite like it? The ten best-dressed men and women in the country look shabby alongside them.

"If God gives such attention to the appearance of wildflowers—most of which are never even seen—don't you think he'll attend to you, take pride in you, do his best for you? What I'm trying to do here is to get you to relax, to not be so preoccupied with getting, so you can respond to God's giving. People who don't know God and the way he works fuss over these things, but you know both God and how he works. Steep your life in God-reality, God-initiative, God-provisions. Don't worry about missing out. You'll find all your everyday human concerns will be met. Give your entire attention to what God is doing right now, and don't get worked up about what may or may not happen tomorrow. God will help you deal with whatever hard things come up when the time comes" **Matthew 6:25-32 (The Message)**

This sounds like the same message God the Creator gave Adam and Eve.

This doesn't necessarily mean our bank accounts will always be overflowing. It doesn't mean we will be free to buy every version of the Apple Watch. We might not get to travel to Europe every year or ever. What it does mean is everything we actually need, we will get moment by moment, as we actually need it. " Give us this day our daily bread…"

And my God will meet all your needs according to the riches of his glory in Christ Jesus.
Philippians 4:19

Here is a quick summary of the some of the areas of your life being supplied. Let's start with the obvious and move to the less obvious.

Financial capital: We have some measure of resources to spend, save, and give.

Intellectual capital: We have intellectual abilities and a vast array of knowledge.

Physical capital: We have time and energy and a physical body that is beyond amazing.

Relational capital: We have relational equity and love available to invest in the quantity and quality of our relationships.

Spiritual capital: We have faith, wisdom, power, love and much more, to use in experiencing and expressing the kingdom of God here and now.

(For more information on the "Five Capitals" be sure to download our friend's book, "Build a Better Life: Practical Tools and Strategies to Develop and Lead Your Life and Business the Way Jesus Would, " by Brandon Schaefer.)

The Entitlement Trap

We have so much yet, we still want more.

We feel entitled to a great vacation after a hard year on the job. Or, it has been, as in our case, ten years since we've had a new car. We think, "We deserve a newer model."

Our list of wants is endless.

Between super savvy marketing and the barrage of ads everywhere from subways, to buses, to taxis to billboards, to panel trucks to pop up ads to magazines and email we are constantly challenged to want more and more and more.

Entitlement for adults and kids is a huge problem. The message to keep up with the culture is relentless. The push and pull of want and need, dissatisfaction and acquiring is rampant.

When we desire what others have we have fallen for the oldest trick in the tempter's book. It is a lie that we deserve this special treatment or that luxury or that we have really missed out until we've been there and done that.

Sometimes, as it has been for us, it takes losing most all your earthly possessions to finally discover the treasure that can't be taken away.

The things we fear most, loss and death, ultimately bring us - if we are willing - true abundance and the reality that everything, even the worst things, can always become new in God.

Would that you could grasp this truth just from the hearing of it- without having to actually go through a fire, or divorce, or unemployment or cancer or major accident. But we're not sure that's possible, or at least it won't stay with you very long – we are a stubborn and stupid people. We keep reaching and grasping and accumulating until we finally – hopefully before it's too late - wake up to see that what we counted on was never fully there.

So, learn to recognize the subtle and not so subtle drivers of fear, prestige, pleasure and greed that draw you toward grasping and neediness. See all your Heavenly Father supplies you right this minute that meets and exceeds your deepest desires for peace, joy and love. It's all there. Open your eyes, your heart, and your arms and receive it.

We all live off his generous bounty, gift after gift after gift.
John 1:16

Chapter 15

Meaningful Purpose

Success, when it does come, tends to be relatively short-lived. That means that we're all thrown back on ourselves sooner or later. When that day arrives we have no choice but to find something more lasting to pin our hopes on.

Scott London

We believe you were designed to have meaningful purpose, to represent the love of the family of God in your own unique way wherever you happen to be in the world. Sounds wonderfully exotic, doesn't it? But so often we seem unhappy in our efforts to accomplish our purpose. We question if we have done enough. Or we have incredibly high standards and we see others rising "higher" so we amp ourselves up to meet or to beat them.

One thing we know for sure, whatever it is we do, there will always be the temptation to believe we must do more.

If you work in the medical field, there are always more patients to see.

As a parent there are never enough hours to build into your child all you think they need for their lives, happiness and future success.

If you work in sales there are always competitors to keep up with and sales quotas meet. There are always more degrees to obtain for further success in your chosen field.

If spiritual ministry is your life work, the Great Commission of Jesus looms ever before you to "Go into all the world and preach the good news..."

So the going never stops.

One reason we do this may be that our true, pure motives are mixed with a subconscious need to cover some kind of guilt.

In the beginning God gave the first couple specific things to achieve so they could partner with the heavenly community to accomplish what it desires to see happen on earth. There was work without strife. There was achievement without burnout.

> God blessed them and said to them, "Be fruitful and increase in number; fill the earth and subdue it. Rule over the fish in the sea and the birds in the sky and over every living creature that moves on the ground."
> **Genesis 1:28**

> The Lord God took the man and put him in the Garden of Eden to work it and take care of it.
> **Genesis 2:15**

God in essence said: I've created you to enjoy relationship with me and also to care for the place I've put you in on this earth. I'm equipping you for responsibilities and stewardship of all I've given you. And I want you to grow and expand it as my representative.

God gave Adam and Eve work to do...
- NOT so they could "earn their keep"...
- NOT so they could prove that they were worthy...
- NOT so they could earn God's favor...
- NOT so they could demonstrate their significance...

The first couple woke each day to lavish love from God and one another, abundant supply, and something meaningful to achieve.

God's early intent was to co-labor with Adam and Eve. They were to bring their humanity to God's divine plan. He wanted their contribution. But it wasn't all up to them. God knew the limitations of human effort but he invited their partnership just the same.

pg. 82

Our True Identity

Genesis 1:26-31, Luke 3:21-22

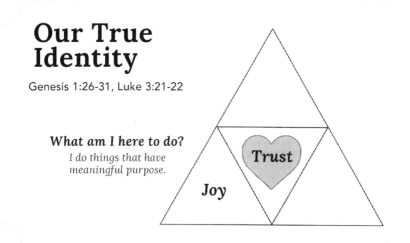

What am I here to do?
*I do things that have
meaningful purpose.*

Trust

Joy

Each day God has given us something to do, too. We know, from scripture what part of our assignment is to be but God also directs us through how we've been wired and created, by what inspires us, what impassions us, what fulfills us, what we are good at.

- What moves you to action?
- What do you dream about doing in service to the world?
- What makes sense for you do in light of your unique wiring and gifts?
- What field is God inviting you to cultivate as his representative?

We see God being represented so often through the gifts of our friends. Clark and David are amazing at remodeling houses. Nancy inspires leaders and creates meaningful spiritual experiences for people throughout the world. Kent oversees people who nurture thousands of acres of vegetables each year. Phillip cares for his clients and the earth through landscaping. Our doctor friends, Wendy, Karim, and Ann have been given the field of medicine to cultivate and expand for the family of God.

But how do we do our work well without powering up into striving mode?

Again, Jesus gives us some clues.

*At that time Jesus came from Nazareth in Galilee and was baptized
by John in the Jordan. Just as Jesus was coming up out of the water,
he saw heaven being torn open and the Spirit descending on him*

like a dove and a voice came from heaven: "You are my Son, whom
I love; with you I am well pleased."
Mark 1:9-11

The word from heaven on Jesus is "I am well pleased with you." Again, Jesus has done nothing notable. He has not healed anyone. He has not spoken the first word to the multitudes. He hasn't fed the masses. But, God is already smiling.

This totally messes with us. We live in a work-for-reward culture. The more hours you put in the more folks love you. We try to be impressive in hopes of earning "well done." Eventually we learn that the treadmill of achievement and power brings no lasting satisfaction. It might bring a nice pay check but where is the lasting satisfaction and fulfillment? Because it's a treadmill and there is always a higher mark to hit, exhaustion is part of the picture that never goes away... Unless we learn to view achievement through the long-term lens of God's pleasure with us. This can't be added to or taken away no matter how high up we go in our company, or how many albums we sell, or how many hits we get on YouTube.

The example we have from Jesus, who is our map for our human experience, is that our heavenly dad is already and forever impressed with us. God is 'predisposed to be pleased with us always. Jesus shows us that taking huge hills in hopes of gaining God's (or someone else's) attention is a total waste of our time and effort. Finally, we see we are free to bring the best of what we've been made to do instead of doing things to prove that we're the best.

Our True Identity

Genesis 1:26-31, Luke 3:21-22

Who am I?
I'm lavishly loved as I am

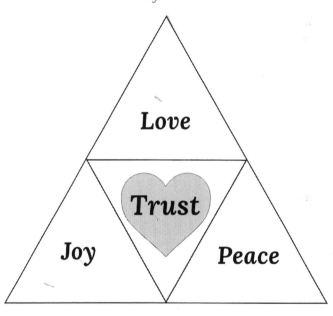

What am I here to do?
*I do things that have
meaningful purpose*

How much do I have?
*I have sufficient supply
for what I need*

Chapter 16

Integrating Your Two Identities

Transformational knowing of self always involves encountering and embracing previously unwelcomed parts of self. While we tend to think of ourselves as a single, unified self, what we call, "I" is really a family of many part selves. That in it self is not a particular problem. The problem lies in the fact that many of these selves are unknown to us. Even though others usually know them, we remain blissfully oblivious of their existence.

David Benner

This might be a good time to tackle the obvious question: how can we enjoy the life we were born to live if we always have two different drivers steering us in opposite directions?

It seems like we have known forever that each of us has an "old nature" at war with a "new nature." We thought it was our job to wipe out all signs of that old nature in order to live a truly abundant life. Out with the old, in with the new, right? What we're learning is that it is our denial and shunning of our old nature that actually gives us the most trouble relationally, emotionally, spiritually and morally.

Hang with us on this.

We never fully live out of just one of our identities. We are always a mixture of both with a continual goal toward wholeness. And coming to see ourselves as we truly are is crucial to becoming whole.

Here's how David explains a significant encounter with this:

I was sitting out on our back porch one Sunday morning, three or four months after my resignation. It felt odd and unsettling that I was alone on a Sunday instead of leading the vibrant spiritual community we had pastored for decades. As I was sitting there in misery, shame, and guilt, I asked the Lord what he wanted me to be aware of at that moment. Almost instantly I got a picture in my mind of a large banquet table with people sitting around it. My sense was, I was sitting at one end of the table and God was sitting at the other end.

As I looked closer, the Lord seemed to say: "David, here are all the different parts of you."

And as I looked at that table I could see:
my leadership self
my relational self
my successful self
my humorous self
my loving self
my generous self
my efficient self
my God- loving self

I also saw less desirable parts of me:
my selfish self
my impatient self
my exhausted self
my intense self

As I looked around the table, I sensed the Lord say: "David… these are the parts of yourself you have allowed at your table. Now, I want you to invite the other parts, the ones you kept hidden from yourself."

Tears came to my eyes. I knew what God was asking of me and it felt excruciating.

With some reluctance, I visually "invited" to the table all the shunned parts of myself I had denied:

   my deceptive self

   my approval-seeking self

   my angry self

   my unfaithful self

As I invited the most repugnant parts of me to the table, it was like I could see my accepted parts making faces at them. They seemed disgusted, embarrassed and irritated that they were being asked to move over and make room for these low-life intruders.

Then the Lord said: "Now, we are all finally here. While I have known each part of you throughout your lifetime, you have denied these unseemly parts exist. But, I have loved every part of you. I have seen every part in all its glory and it's garbage.. I don't see good and bad, acceptable and unacceptable parts. I just see you. Now I'm inviting you to acknowledge all the parts of you around this table. I want you to extend love and compassion to every part, just like I do."

So, with tears streaming down my face I surrendered to what God was asking and welcomed each part of myself to the table of my life. If he could accept them and love them, I could learn to do that too.

Jesus teaches integration of the whole person this way:

> The kingdom of heaven is like a man who sowed good seed in his field. But while everyone was sleeping, his enemy came and sowed weeds among the wheat and went away. When the wheat sprouted and formed heads, then the weeds also appeared. The owner's servants came to him and said, "Sir, didn't you sow good seed in your field? Where then did the weeds come from?"
>
> "An enemy did this," he replied.
>
> The servants asked him, "Do you want us to go and pull them up?"
>
> "No," he answered, "because while you are pulling the weeds, you

may uproot the wheat with them. Let both grow together until the harvest. At that time I will tell the harvesters: First collect the weeds and tie them in bundles to be burned; then gather the wheat and bring it into my barn."
Matthew 13:24-30

Our lives do not consist of wheat or weeds, heavenly revelations or hellish experiences. We are always and continuously a confounding combination of both. The Apostle Paul confirms this too.

For if I know the law but still can't keep it, and if the power of sin within me keeps sabotaging my best intentions, I obviously need help! I realize that I don't have what it takes. I can will it, but I can't do it. I decide to do good, but I don't really do it; I decide not to do bad, but then I do it anyway. My decisions, such as they are, don't result in actions. Something has gone wrong deep within me and gets the better of me every time. **Romans 7: 18-23 (The Message)**

It happens so regularly it's predictable. The moment we decide to do good, sin is there to trip us up. We truly delight in God's commands, but it's pretty obvious not every part of us joins in that delight. Parts of us covertly, subconsciously rebel, and just when we least expect it, they take over.

This happens in all of us - whether we can admit it or not - but for the purposes of our story David had dis-owned and dis-associated himself from his most undesirable parts. He could not face them. They could not be part of someone who was so committed to God and loved his wife. Failure has always been David's worst nightmare. So when he failed, whether it was in leadership, financially or morally he did what all of us do, he compartmentalized the ugly parts into tightly locked internal "rooms." He didn't know it at the time, but the way he compartmentalized allowed deception to grow.

In the past, whenever David experienced major tension between the wheat and weeds in his life, his solution was to keep the good and the bad separated and walled off from each other. One side couldn't see the other. This created a split in his experience of self and resulted in one part of him growing an ability to tolerate sin.

Where Two or More Are Gathered

One healthy way to integrate all the dimensions of your life is to find a "safe community" of one to three people you can be brutally honest with... about every part of the good, bad, and ugly of your life - a community where you don't have to put on any kind of mask, performance or persona.

The goal would be to gather this tight group of unconditionally loving friends for the purpose of sharing your whole self, to create an atmosphere of deep trust where there is nothing to prove. Success for this group is when everyone feels on equal footing with the knowledge that there will be no judgment, withdrawal or repercussions from whatever is shared.

From our own experience and from comments of friends and fellow ministers over the years a group like this is extremely rare for most people but, especially, for senior pastors and their wives. There are a whole host of reasons for this. But, the inability of these leaders to find a safe place to fully share themselves puts this group at particularly high risk for isolation, discouragement, burnout, depression and moral failure.

From our experience, the solution isn't about finding more iron clad ways to hold someone's "feet to the fire." It's about holding a compassionate space in our hearts for others to feel safe enough to share the unvarnished truth of their real life experiences.

Side bar with David:

You may be wondering how I could have been married, leading a church and engaged in infidelity. It's an utterly valid question. One I ask myself on a regular basis. It seems unthinkable to me now. I lived the vast amount of time from the wholeness in Christ I taught others to seek but there were times I slipped into brokenness. That devastated me and in anguish I confessed my sin to God.

The problem was I never felt safe enough to confess my failure to someone else. Had I found a safe place, I am convinced the spell of denial that allowed me to do this would have instantly been broken. One reason we hide our dark sides in spiritual communities can be traced to the Reformation. That's right. That great movement by Martin Luther that brought many sweeping changes desperately needed in the church. Until that time, people had been taught that in order for their sins to be forgiven they had to confess to a priest.

The Reformation enlightened everyone about the scriptures, and people realized it was their confession to God not to another person that resulted in forgiveness. (Later, many would come to realize we are already forgiven, even before we confess to anyone, including God.)

However, this stance on confession, while well intended, seemed to ignore James 5:16 - *"Therefore confess your sins to each other and pray for each other so that you may be healed."* At the time of the reformation the baby of confession to one another was thrown out with the bathwater of confession to priests. This is a generalization, I know, but most Protestants pride themselves in not needing a priest for confession, and in only confessing their sins to God.

A huge part of being healed from our brokenness is found in bringing our failures into the light before non-condemning sisters and brothers. There is great power in admitting our unseemly parts in the presence of a loving, wise, and trusting counselor, spiritual director, or group. This IS the good news of Jesus. We see him model for us the acceptance of every kind of unpleasant, unacceptable person on nearly every page of the gospels. Yet, most Christian communities are still not equipped to respond with true biblical grace, compassion and restoration particularly when spiritual leaders confess sin. So often we respond to them like a deer in headlights then we show our otherwise faithful, seasoned soldiers the door. Just like we do with our own inner darkness, churches deny, shun and expel failed leaders in clumsy, but well meaning attempts to remove the sin from their midst.

So, what do we do with failed Christian leaders?

Some might say, at best, it is complicated. We think it could not be clearer if we have the courage to follow the words and ways of our True Leader. Regardless of the complications, what we do know is that our error to offer grace and compassion to any Christ-follower only serves to drive their secrets even further into hiding and away from healing light.

We do not reflect our Savior or serve our churches when we:

1) Make failed leaders exceptions to the common grace and fellowship of Christ

2) Reject and exile fully repentant leaders

3) Do not make complete restoration to the body of Christ where the failure took place our ultimate goal.

Darkness must be brought into the light in order for us to be healed. Secrets must be exposed to others for God to do his full work. In my case, it was completely necessary for my healing, for the greatest failure of my life to be revealed to my wife and a small circle of humble, grace-filled leaders fully aware of and in touch with their own brokenness.

We do not believe it brings healing to anyone that their sin be publicly exposed, unless the guilty party himself or herself decides a public confession is necessary. It is not our job to bring humiliation, condemnation and judgment on others, but to cover them, forgive them, help heal them and restore them. The scriptures are replete with this mandate. Yet, I do understand the confusion on these matters.

In the 1980's, I, myself, led in the public "discipline" of a man in our church who had sinned*. At the time, the approach we took seemed like the right thing to do. Hindsight often painfully reveals there are higher ways of relating and behaving toward those who have hurt, deceived and disappointed us without dismissing the truth. Yet, sending people into exile for "uncleanness" was something Jesus definitively and demonstratively taught against.

(*Let me add here, so there is no misunderstanding: if there has been illegal behavior of any kind we should and are required by law to notify the authorities.)

Living In Denial

In my situation, another big reason I could not bring my failure into the light, was because I was hiding it from myself. I never called the situation what it actually was. As weird as this sounds I never saw it as an "affair." And I never thought of the relationship in terms of "love" so it was not, in my deceived mind, ever in competition with our marriage. I clearly knew I had failed. But, most of the time the "unthinkableness" of my sin kept it blocked from my active consciousness which enabled me to function as if nothing untoward had happened.

It usually takes something very dramatic to shock us awake when we are in denial. This is why we say when some severe loss, pain, betrayal, or failure occurs we have a chance to further awaken to our significant inner drivers.

Sin always proceeds from lack of awareness. Most of us are just not aware and not fully living in our own present moment. When Jesus said, "Father, forgive them, they don't know what they're doing" (Luke 23:34), he was absolutely right. Most people are on cruise control, and most of their reactions are habituated brain responses--not completely thought out choices.

We avoid reality and the depth of our own souls because big truths initially disturb our comfortable, small self.

Spiritual maturity is to finally become aware that we are not the entire persona (mask) we have been presenting to others. To grow we must become more intentional about recognizing and embracing our shadows.

There is no shortage of opportunities to discover our shadow. As Carl Jung says, *"Everything that irritates us about others can lead us to an understanding of ourselves."* Jung sees the forgiving ("integrating") of our shadow self as an essential task of every person.

What's important is that once I owned my shadow side as well as owned my legitimate need for safety, understanding and peace, new breakthroughs began emerging. I now own everything that is true about me as soon as I can be aware of it and I'm learning, to become quicker and more accurate at noticing and offering compassion to the very human, unacceptable parts of me. This is truly a personal breakthrough.

Richard Rohr has said, *"What we don't own will end up owning us."* The more we stuff hurts, needs, failures, loss, etc., the stronger they will grow over time. They eventually "act out" and when they do, it's not pretty. When we hide from our weaknesses we are disassociating ourselves from complete reality. It's our way of trying to manage our reality but it's an unhealthy and dangerous way of coping.

Chapter 17

Embracing Imperfection

*We must bear patiently not being good and
not being thought good.*

Francis of Assisi

Another influence that impacts our ability to fully integrate our lives is a theology of spiritual perfection. For most of us, our spirituality has been focused on outward performance, willpower, and achievement. Some people have referred to this as a "ladder theology" which has dominated much of church history.

Jesus speaks to this in Luke 18:

To some who were confident of their own righteousness and looked down on everyone else, Jesus told this parable: "Two men went up to the temple to pray, one a Pharisee and the other a tax collector. The Pharisee stood by himself and prayed: 'God, I thank you that I am not like other people—robbers, evildoers, adulterers—or even like this tax collector. I fast twice a week and give a tenth of all I get.' "But the tax collector stood at a distance. He would not even look up to heaven, but beat his breast and said, 'God, have mercy on me, a sinner.' "I tell you that this man, rather than the other, went home justified before God. For all those who exalt themselves will be humbled, and those who humble themselves will be exalted.

The Pharisees were always seen as the good guys who were desperately trying to do everything right. The tax collectors were hated because they took money from the Jewish people and turned it over to the Romans.

Jesus' set-up in this story is brilliant. Everyone admires the Pharisees and despises the tax collectors.

The surprise reveal in the story was that the Pharisee believed he had done everything right… followed all the rules… and was so full of himself that he didn't have room for God. But it was the hated tax collector who admitted he was a sinner. And Jesus shocked the crowd by saying the tax collector is more "righteous" than the Pharisee!

It makes more sense to our finite human minds that the Sinless Son of God would steer clear of anything less than perfect. But, Jesus was totally attracted to messed up, shameful people. That is not a misprint.

The sickly, unseemly people got his attention. Blind eyes, deaf ears, and outcasts – did not repel him, they compelled him. He preferred to dine with the destitute, call on the crippled and welcome the wayward. The baddest man in the region? Jesus is headed to his house. A compromised woman with perfume? He says, I'll make that girl famous.

Jesus doesn't badmouth our brokenness. Even, if we should have known better. Then, why is it that when the sorry shambles of our lives break public, we think we're done? Or, if someone we know turns up tainted, we run? Where did we learn this?

Jesus is a lover and gatherer of the broken, splintered pieces of what was our lives (get this: even if it used to be known far and wide as an exemplary, lovely Christ-honoring life) and like a master artisan; he will find a way to refit and restore what is left into something surprising, breathtaking, and new. God gives beauty for ashes and gladness for tears. And from all those nasty shards he makes something so purely whole that it shows off his glory like streaming sunlight through an old, stained-glass window.

So, don't deny your brokenness. Confess it. Repent of it. And offer it to God. As crazy as it sounds, and as impossible as it may look, what you've got is fresh material for a masterpiece.

The Spirit of the Lord is upon me. Because he did anoint me; to proclaim good news to the poor, sent me to heal the broken of heart,

*to proclaim to captives deliverance. And to the blind, receiving of
sight, to send away the bruised with deliverance.*
Luke 4:18 (YLT)

Richard Rohr states it this way: "*Imperfection is the organizing principle
of the entire human, historical, and spiritual enterprise. Imperfection, in
the great spiritual traditions, is not just to be tolerated, excused, or even
forgiven. It is the very framework inside of which God makes the god-
self known (to us) and calls us into gracious union. It's what allows us and
sometimes forces us to fall into the arms of the living God.*"

Some part of you may react to this because you're thinking: "Wait just
a minute. Didn't Jesus tell us in Matthew 5:48 to be perfect just as our
heavenly Father is perfect?" Yes, he did. But what does this "perfect"
mean?

An egotistic, moral-based mind, uses scriptures like this one as a
mathematical mandate for humanity. This then leads people to head-
based, black and white, good or bad thinking that results in pretending,
splitting, and denial. Everyone loses with this since none of us will ever be
perfect.

God's acceptance of our weakness never lessens his desire for our
wholeness.

Another way of viewing this scripture and others like it is that it sets a
very high bar no one can ever achieve on their own. The real goal is not
private perfection but divine union. When you've experienced any level of
divine union or connectedness you know that you have been chosen and
loved even in your imperfection.

Rohr goes on to state "*a spiritually mature person could use the word
perfection and know they are talking about God's perfect abiding in
us. An immature and still egocentric person will think of it as a moral
achievement that they can personally attain by trying harder.*"

So in light of this now, consider the meaning of these verses.
*I no longer seek any perfection from my own efforts... but only the
perfection that comes from faith and is from God... We who are*

called perfect must all think in this way…
Philippians 3:9,15

When I am weak, then I am strong.
2 Corinthians 12:10

Paul again seems to have a spirituality of imperfection, but this has not been the experience of most of Christian history.

Sustainable integration happens when we turn from trying so hard to be good or act good or look good and accept our imperfections trusting God to use them and remove them as we trust in his wholeness, his purity and his righteousness.

We say we know it is all grace and all God, yet we still hold each other and ourselves by a standard even God Himself does not hold for us.

God has chosen to love the human, the ordinary, our imperfect world, an imperfect us. Even more counterintuitive is that God seems to actually use and find necessary for our growth the very things we fear, avoid, deny, and seem as unworthy. This blows our minds!

We are finally able to come to a transformational knowing of ourselves by discovering how we are unconditionally known and loved by God.

So a truly "perfect" person ends up being one who can consciously forgive and include imperfection rather than one who thinks he or she is totally above and beyond it.

You come to God not by being strong, but by being weak; not by being right, but through your mistakes; not by self-admiration but by self-forgetfulness. We know… this is shocking! And yet it shouldn't be. Both Jesus and the Apostle Paul lived and taught us this.

This is the very, very good news of the gospel. When you have faced your own imperfection and impurity and unwillingness to love then you are actually ready to believe that the gospel means that God loves, forgives and transforms all… including (gulp) the "bad guys."

We are learning to hold the mixture of both the dark and the light sides of ourselves in the compassionate way our Heavenly dad does.

Author Hugh Prather has said, *"Forgiveness doesn't excuse behavior; it looks past it to a greater truth."*

There is no excusing what happened to us. But it has been fully and profusely confessed, wept over, investigated and profoundly owned. Now, all that's left is to live into a much greater truth.

Step #3

Participate in the Rhythms of Your Ultimate Identity

The ability to enjoy the life you were born to live comes when you learn to experience yourself right now, settled in peace, in God's loving presence. Without establishing this critical connection your striving for recognition and relationship will never cease.

What can become transformative for you is when you awaken to a deep intuition that you are already participating in something very good, that someone else has already initiated and it is happening right now.

Chapter 18

The Transformer in You

The little mind is always feeling something.
But I am called to address who I am, not how I feel.

Hugh Prather

At some point you probably noticed those large gray boxes or cylinders high on telephone poles called transformers. We call them transformers because that's what they do. On one side of the box powerful, destructive energy comes in, gets absorbed and converted then it shoots out the other side to homes and businesses in safe, useable electric watts. Raw, dangerous power is changed to useful, manageable electricity through that transformer box.

This is one way of picturing what Jesus has done for every one of us.

> *For I didn't send my son in the world to condemn the world but that*
> *the world might be saved through him.*
> **John 3:17**

The operative word is through. At the cross Jesus acts as our transformer. He absorbs sin, wrong and evil and instead of passing it on to others in vengeance, he absorbs it into his body. Then he converts that darkness into positive light. He changes death to life, crucifixion to resurrection and massive loss into enormous gain.

At the cross Jesus looks like a failure. He is rejected, mocked, naked, and disapproved of by everyone. But it is there he absorbs shame and transforms it into love on our behalf.

You no longer have to carry your shame. It has been absorbed and transformed by Jesus.

> *Instead of your shame you will receive a double portion, and instead of disgrace you will rejoice in your inheritance. And so you will inherit a double portion in your land, and everlasting joy will be yours.*
> Isaiah 61:7

At the cross Jesus becomes needy. He says, *"I need a drink."* He absorbs our fear of not having enough and transforms it into abundance. *"He became poor so that we might become rich"* (2 Corinthians 8:9). He makes a pathway for us to move away from fear into peace. You no longer have to carry fear in you because *"his perfect love casts out fear"* (I John 4:18).

At the cross Jesus becomes weak and powerless for our sake. He absorbs our guilt and transforms it so we can live in his power and discover life's greatest force for good; representing the kingdom of God in our own unique way here on earth.

You no longer have to be burdened by guilt because Jesus replaced your weakness, for all time, with his strength.

From Temptation to Transformation

In the desert Jesus resisted three temptations: to be more, to have more, to do more. At the cross he absorbs and transforms them so we can live free. God accounts to us everything he sees in Jesus, even if we have failed or wandered, been destructive or doubted.

Here are three simple ways to experience the Transformer:

Every time you have compulsive, shame thoughts that say:
"You should feel shame because you are not worthy. Something is wrong with you... you're so defective..."

Remind yourself that 95% of your shame-filled thoughts are floating untransformed in your unconscious. They are not who you truly are.

Say to yourself:

"There is nothing wrong with me. At the moment, I am a perfect spiritual being having an imperfect human experience. I am in complete connection with Jesus Christ. What is true of Him has been made true of me. Just as there is no shame in Him, there is no shame in me, because of the transformation of the cross. Jesus recovered what has been true about me from the beginning - I am lavishly loved as I am. His love resides in me and is what is most true of me this day."

Every time you have compulsive, fearful thoughts that say to you:

"Be very afraid. You will never have enough. You are going to run out of (friends, money, information, fun experiences)...you better get anxious because things are about to get bad. "

Remind yourself that 95% of all fearful-filled thoughts happen automatically and they are just temporary imperfect experiences we're having. They are not who you truly are.

Repeat to yourself:

"Everything is going to be ok. At the moment, I am a perfect spiritual being having an imperfect human experience. I am in complete union with Jesus Christ and what's true of Him is true of me. Just as there is no fear in Him, there is no fear in me, because of the transformation of the cross. Jesus has recovered what has been true for me all along - I have sufficient supply for what I need today. His peace is what resides in me and is most true of me this day."

Every time you have compulsive, guilty thoughts that say:

"You should feel bad. There is so much more you could be doing...you need to achieve more... accomplish more... do more for others. You could do so much better. You know all that stuff you've done that you need to make up for."

Remind yourself that 95% of your guilt-laden thoughts happen automatically and they are just temporary imperfect experiences you're having. They do not reflect who you truly are.

pg. 104

Repeat to yourself:

"Slow down. At the moment, I am a perfect spiritual being having an imperfect human experience. I am in complete union with Jesus Christ and what's true of Him is true of me. Just as there is no guilt in Him, there is no guilt in me, because of the transformation of the cross. Jesus has come and recovered what has been true about me all along- I have meaningful purpose for my life. My gifts are active and valuable and helpful to others. What I do or accomplish is no indication of who I truly am. God's unchanging joy resides in me and flows from me. This is what is most true of me this day."

Chapter: 19

The Enneagram: A Tool for Transformation

With the Ennegram it's a matter of inner work that can lend authencity to our spiritual path. At the same time the Enneagram creates new difficulties. Many of our unquestioned assumptions and subliminal solutions can no longer function as they used to.

The Enneagram shows us, among other things, the dark side of our gifts. We are destroyed by our gifts because we identify too closely with what we can do well.

Richard Rohr and Andrea Ebert

The "profile" our counselors used with us and referred to in chapter one is called the Enneagram (pronounced "enny-a-gram"). We had been introduced to the Enneagram several years previous and were just beginning to get our sea legs using it with the staff of our church and with ourselves when it became necessary for us to resign.

At that time, we thought we had a pretty good understanding of what the Enneagram offered. But after spending over a year in weekly sessions digesting it with our counselors we saw we had barely made its acquaintance. Rich and Jim were able to help us determine with pinpoint accuracy several debilitating blind spots that had tripped us up our entire lives.

Though we had taken all the standard personality tests over the years and been somewhat helped by their findings, the Enneagram has far and away offered us the most profound insight into each other and ourselves. It is a tool we still use every day to help us catch our own compulsive thoughts and behavior in action. We became so impacted by its astounding ability to help transform our distorted perceptions of ourselves that we doubled down our efforts to study it and eventually became certified Enneagram specialists.

What Is the Enneagram?

In their comprehensive book, The Enneagram A Christian Perspective Richard Rohr and Adreas Ebert say this about the Enneagram:

The Enneagram has emerged as a tool that is forcing many of us to a brutal and converting honesty about good and evil and the ways we hide from ourselves and therefore hide from God. It tries to address this "compromise with life" and "evasion of reality" that the ego is so invested in... The Enneagram is about the disguise that we all are. The Enneagram is more than an entertaining game for learning about oneself. It is concerned with change and making a turnaround with what the religious traditions call conversion or repentance. It confronts us with compulsions and laws, which we live by-usually without being aware of it—and it aims to invite us to go beyond them, to take steps into the domain of freedom.

The Enneagram can help us purify our self-perceptions, to become unsparingly honest toward ourselves, and to discern better and better when we are hearing only our own inner voices and impressions and are prisoners of our prejudices...The Enneagram does not have the intention of flattering or stroking the "empirical ego. "Rather it aims to support efforts to let go of or render unnecessary what Thomas Merton calls the "false self.' I know no other means of achieving this more directly than the Enneagram.

We include some very basic Enneagram information in this book because nothing else we have ever used has come close to helping us see our compulsive patterns with such clarity. We also believe when it is used along with trained coaching or counseling, this tool offers the best chance for lasting personal, spiritual and relational transformation. These are pretty bold statements, we know. Our experience with it has been that life-changing.

The Enneagram will invite you to celebrate your true self, the unique way in which you bear the image of God, as well as challenge you to engage in the transformation of your calculating self, which prevents you from fully being who God has designed and gifted you to be.

The following can act as an introductory map that can guide you in self-reflection. It can help you understand how you tend to sort information and relate to others. When studied in-depth, with the help of a guide well versed in this tool, The Enneagram can act as a codebook, to help you understand your own wiring patterns and those of others.

This map of nine specific types of personality, can demonstrate for you what is virtuous in you and what is a temptation to falsely act as your compulsive identity.

The power of this tool is that it helps you discover the roots of what prevents you from living, loving, and leading from the Source of your true identity. It can show you the root of your suffering; the place of your greatest temptation to sin and the true gifts you bring to the world.

A fabulous thing about the Enneagram is that it takes what is unconscious in us and helps us see it for what it is. Each of the roots of these nine types are the specific ways in which we forget who we really are and our sense of connection with God.

Here is just a very brief overview of the nine types. You'll probably recognize parts of you in many of the types, but you need to know that one of them is probably what is most dominant and influential in you. And, it is often said; the one type we most do not want to be is probably our dominant type.

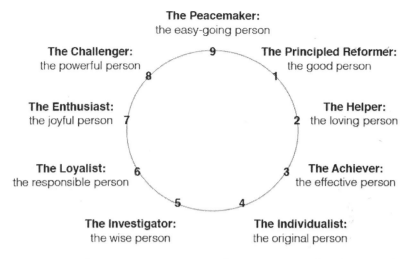

The Enneagram: Nine different views of reality

The Peacemaker:
the easy-going person

The Challenger:
the powerful person

The Principled Reformer:
the good person

The Enthusiast:
the joyful person

The Helper:
the loving person

The Loyalist:
the responsible person

The Achiever:
the effective person

The Investigator:
the wise person

The Individualist:
the original person

Three types that perceive reality primarily through their feelings and battle with SHAME:

Type Two: The Helper/The Loving Person.

- This person is able to lovingly use their gifts to serve the needs of others. They represent the caring, loving nature of God.

- This person is desperate to be liked. They have a fear of worthlessness if they aren't feeling useful. Their great temptation is to compulsively help and serve others to the point of ignoring their own needs, then becoming resentful and, eventually, they burn out.

- Their invitation to transformation is in the area of: Pride

- Their compulsive identity says: "I am helpful."

Type Three: The Achiever/The Effective Person

- This person is able to be productive and ambitious. They are able to accomplish many things. They represent the leadership and effectiveness of God.

- This person is desperate to look good, to be seen as successful. They fear failure. Their great temptation is to continually create a put together image that looks good and can be 'sold' or believed in, thus they deceive themselves and others by projecting they are more than they truly are.

- Their invitation to transformation is in the area of: Self-deception

- Their compulsive identity says: "I am successful."

Type Four: The Individualist/The Original Person

- This person is able to be creative, imaginative, stylish and original. They represent the creative, sensitive nature of God.

- This person is desperate to be different, special and unique. They fear being ordinary. Their great temptation is to continually compare themselves to others, which can lead them to moodiness and depression.

- Their invitation to transformation is in the area of: Envy

- Their compulsive identity says: "I am special."

Three types that perceive reality primarily through their minds and battle with FEAR:

Type Five: The Investigator/The Wise Person

- This person is able to be curious, perceptive, and ever-growing in knowledge. They represent the wise, all knowing God.

- This person is desperate to feel fulfilled. They fear being helpless and incapable in relationships. Their great temptation is to avoid emotional or relational engagement, which can lead them to feeling empty.

- Their invitation to transformation is in the area of: Greed (to gain and hoard - especially knowledge.)

- Their compulsive identity says: "I am perceptive."

Type Six: The Loyalist/The Responsible Person

- This person is able to be a reliable, cooperative team player and a loyal, warmhearted friend. They represent the responsibility of a faithful God.

- This person is desperate to feel more secure. They can easily succumb to self-doubt and pessimism. Their great temptation is to cave into anxiety.

- Their invitation to transformation is in the area of: Anxiety/fear

- Their compulsive identity says: "I am the guardian of_____"

Type Seven: The Enthusiast/The Joyful Person

- This person is able to have infectious humor and enjoys adventure. They represent the enthusiastic, joy-filled God.

- This person is desperate not to feel pain. They have difficulty dealing with the emotional problems of themselves and others. Their great temptation is to master the art of bluffing.

- Their initiation to transformation is in the area of: Gluttony (appetite for more of something)

- Their compulsive identity says: "I am OK."

Three types who perceive reality primarily through their intuition and battle with GUILT:

Type Eight: The Challenger/The Powerful Person

- This person is able to impress others as strong and influential. They love challenging people and the status quo. They represent the strong and powerful God.

- This person is desperate not to look weak. They are fearful of being harmed or controlled by others. Their great temptation is to not admit mistakes.

- Their invitation to transformation is in the area of: Forcefulness

- Their compulsive identity says: "I am powerful."

Type Nine: The Peacemaker/The Easy Going Person

- This person is able to accept others without prejudice and act as a place of rest for others. They represent the peace of God.

- This person is desperate to avoid conflict. They can tend to be lethargic and too comfortable. Their great temptation is to be passively uncommitted.

- Their invitation to transformation is in the area of: Disengagement/laziness

- Their compulsive identity says: "I am settled."

Type One: The Principled Reformer/The Good Person

- This person is able to have a strong sense of right or wrong and how things should be done. They represent the principled goodness of God.

- This type is desperate to correct everything according to their sense of rightness. They have such high standards that they have a hard time accepting the imperfections of themselves and others. Their great temptation is to be judgmental.

- Their invitation to transformation is in the area of: Resentment/Anger

- Their compulsive identity says: "I am right."

All nine of these personality types are ways in which we've been conditioned to view reality. Your type shows your "point of view" of the world.

It's about this time you might be asking, "What's all this talk about the self? Didn't Jesus tell us to die to ourselves?"

Before our tragedy we believed the whole key to spiritual transformation could be summed up in knowing and following God. Sounds right, doesn't it? But, let's think about that for a minute. Think about people you know who thoroughly believe in God, maybe they go to church regularly and attend Bible studies, maybe they do good things for others but their personal relationships or vocational lives have some pretty significant snags or gaps. While no one is perfect, for all the ways we claim to know about God, our lives should be much better off.

We have discovered it is actually at the intersection of knowing God *and* authentically knowing ourselves that we find genuine, lasting personal transformation.

pg. 112

In his book, *The Gift of Being Yourself: The Sacred Call to Self Discovery*, psychologist and author David Benner says this:

> Christian spirituality involves a transformation of the self that occurs only when God and self are both deeply known. Both therefore have an important place in Christian spirituality. 'There is no deep knowing of God without deep knowing of self,' John Calvin wrote. Thomas a Kempis argued that 'a humble self knowledge is a surer way to God than a search after deep learning' and Augustine's prayer was 'Grant, Lord, that I may know myself that I may know thee.' Nearly the whole of sacred doctrine consist of these two parts; knowledge of God and of ourselves. Yet we have focused on knowing God and tended to ignore knowing ourselves.
>
> The consequences have often been grievous –marriages betrayed, families destroyed, ministries shipwrecked and endless numbers of people damaged. Not all knowledge transforms. Some merely puffs up. Self-knowledge that is pursued apart from knowing our identity in relationship to God leads to self inflation (1Cor 8:1). Knowing God and knowing self are therefore interdependent. Neither can proceed very far without the other.

Here are our options: We can stay asleep to our small self ego that causes us suffering and constricts the life of God residing in us, or we can wake to a much larger reality that lives inside us, the life that is called the Kingdom of God.

Your Personal Inventory

Before you move on to the next chapter, take some time here to review the nine types above and see if you can narrow down which two or three may be your Enneagram type. It often takes some time and self-observation to land the plane on the one that is most fully your type. You will have varying degrees of other types mixed with yours.

Notice which types you find yourself resisting or disliking as you read the descriptions.

There is a natural tendency to pick out types for other people. Try to avoid going there and focus on what actually rings most true for you. Over the next few days and weeks ask God to bring these descriptions to mind as events happen that might bring them to the surface. The point is not to be self-critical but to be self-aware. This practice of awareness will help the unhealthy tendencies of your personality begin to recede.

NOTE: *If you are interested in a much more thorough, expanded understanding of your Enneagram type and the insightful ways it can enhance and help grow every area of your life contact us at youlivetrue. com for information about our Enneagram test and follow up consultation.*

Chapter 20

Cultivating Your True Identity

*We are not human beings having a spiritual experience.
We are spiritual beings having a human experience.*
Pierre Teilhard de Chardin

Before we left that first infamous counseling intensive with Rich and Jim, Caron asked a question all of us ask at some point in our lives. " I am in so much pain. Our life is unrecognizable. How am I expected to get through this? And the answer came back, "The only way we know to get through anything, the only way to ultimate personal healing and transformation is to spend time alone with God in silence resting on his unfailing love."

Well, this is not what Caron wanted to hear. They might as well have said "Go straight to the Empire State Building and stand on your head." She wanted something tangible, a real solution. She was still in shock. Our entire lives were upside down. Even God, who had been so close and familiar had disappeared. It felt laughable that this was the counselor's best shot at a solution.

Now, several years later, neither of us can imagine real help coming in any other way.

Once we learn to see what is actually real, we can truly begin to live.

The material world must fail us in some way so that the spiritual world can be broken open to us. Somehow we must be shaken awake to the false nature of things in order for us to get grounded in the beauty, wonder and joy of what can never perish or be taken away from us.

Our culture has the concept of "reality" backwards. It is not the tangible, temporal things that are real, but only that which is eternal, unending and everlasting. But, this is so counterintuitive. It's what we experience with our five senses that most often seems real. That's why it often takes radical hardship, health issues or loss to finally show us our deeper cries for that which can never fail or harm us.

Once you are convinced God sees you, knows you and approves of you, you can finally relax all your compulsions to be sure everyone else does, too. When you can trust that your Heavenly Parent truly does have your ultimate best in mind at all times, you can begin to let go of your relentless, exhausting drive to control every aspect of your destiny. When you are able to lean on what you cannot see more than you depend on what you can see, you increase your potential for joy and happiness 100-fold.

Richard Rohr says it this way:
> I call the egocentric perspective "the calculating mind," and I call the soul-centric mind perspective "the contemplative mind." The first mind sees everything through the lens of its own private needs and hurts, angers and memories. It is too small a lens to see truthfully, wisely, or deeply.
>
> The contemplative mind is an alternative processing system that is actually a positive widening of your lens for a better picture. It is hard work to learn how to pray this way, largely the work of emptying the mind and filling the heart...the contemplative mind prays from a different sense of who-I-am. It rests and abides in the Great I AM, and draws its life from the Larger Vine (John 15) the Deeper Well (John 4)... Basically prayer is an exercise in divine participation—you opting in and God always there! ... Our willingness to be open to 'conscious contact with God' and to creatively work with the hand that life and sin and circumstance have dealt us is our deepest prayer and truest obedience to God.

Fully trusting a God we cannot see is impossible without vibrant spiritual experiences with God in real time, "conscious contact." Knowledge of

God alone never transforms us. Real change only comes through our actual experiences inside of Great Love.

So, how do we get those experiences?

Though it can tend to sound mystical, part of learning to live true is participating in sacred rhythms that re-align us with the life we really want, the life God originally designed for us to share with him. These rhythms or practices help us experience all God is doing in us, for us and with us right now. They help us to see the utter futility of all our desperate striving to manufacture whole, happy lives on our own.

There are countless spiritual rhythms available to us. We will share two simple, yet profound ones in the next chapter. You just need to discover and practice the ones that most help you uniquely experience your true self in God.

The good news of the gospel is not about being correct... it's about being connected. And being connected as much as possible begins by learning to shift our awareness.

Locate and experience your real identity

We are perfect spiritual beings having imperfect human experiences. When we understand the perfect nature of spiritual being (you are hidden with Christ in God), which is our true, created identity, then we can recognize that everything else that happens to us, in us and around us, is an imperfect human experience.

We recognize our perfect spiritual being... our true, created identity as: *Permanent, Unchanging, Satisfied, Whole, Full, Flexible, Open, Surrendered.*

And our imperfect human experience... our conditioned, compulsive identity is: *Temporary, Changing, Discontent, Broken, Empty, Calculating, Controlling, Defending.*

Your thoughts, emotions, and even your body molecules, come and go. Each day comes and goes. Each season comes and goes. They are mere forms that arrive out of nowhere, make a brief appearance, and then they are gone.

Your core... your true identity has always been there. It is formless. It is the one thing that has been here before anything else, and will be the one thing that remains after all else disappears. The part of you that was present before, during, and after anything and everything else is the real you. If you can learn to shift your most focused awareness away from what keeps passing away to the One who will never leave you, that shift is your ticket to freedom.

The ancient poet, Rumi, is the best selling poet in the United States, and yet he lived in the 12th century. He once posed this provocative question: "Why do you stay in prison when the door is wide open?"

We think the prison he was referring to is our compulsive identities. The way to the lives we've been designed for happens when we learn to shift our most focused awareness away from our compulsive practices and on to what is most everlastingly true.

We began this book with the premise that everything we do, say, think, and how we behave, all comes from who we think we are.

So right now... try to put yourself in a posture of awareness by asking yourself: *"What am I aware of in me right now?"* If the real me is always here, then those other things that come and go, must not be me, but just experiences that I am having. Whenever you notice anything, who is it that is doing the noticing? Who is noticing is what the Bible calls our inner witness---our spirit... the place of our union with God.

Romans 8:16 says: *"The Spirit joins with our spirit to bear common witness that we are children of God."*

In the Message translation it reads: *"God's Spirit touches our spirits and confirms who we really are. We know who he is, and we know who we are: Father and children."*

Now - hang with us - and ask: *"Who is being aware of me being aware?"* Whenever you are stressed in anyway, stop and ask this question. It will bring you into the presence of who you really are. Everything else you are noticing, you can either enjoy it or endure it, but you no longer have to be imprisoned by it.

When you can notice and talk about your thoughts and feelings from the perspective of a detached outsider it helps them become less compulsive. It gives you the ability to actually see what is separate from yourself. They are just thoughts. Feelings. Experiences. But they are not your true self.

When you begin to live from this new place, you no longer have to prove, protect, or promote yourself. Your inner witness (which is in perfect union with God and your True self) begins to notice whenever your automatic patterns occur. That witness can let the false self go and drop back into the kingdom of God within you that now sees and knows actual reality.

Paul says in Philippians 4:7 to *"Pray with gratitude, and the peace of God which is beyond all knowledge, will guard your hearts and minds in Christ Jesus."* Notice he says that the peace of God is a place beyond knowledge, meaning beyond all of our processing of ideas, labels, and information. Then he tells us to guard all that's within us. This is the innermost part of you that is at peace. It is able to 'witness' and calmly watch the flow of your thoughts (mind) and your feelings (heart.)

So here's the deal: God is always observing and loving us compassionately in all our perfection and imperfection... just as we are. Only when our spirit learns how to calmly join with His Spirit do we find the capacity to stand guard and then shift gears.

The goal in all of this is seeing your small, imprisoning, calculating thoughts for what they really are and learning to trust yourself inside the much larger, freeing mind of Christ.

Chapter 21

Two Simple Practices for Personal Transformation

It is in solitude that we recognize, with a shock, how lost we have been, and that now we are found, rescued, recovering conscience, returning to ourselves, to Truth, carried by Him who has sought and found us.

Thomas Merton

Practice #1 - Read the First Bible.

The first Bible ever produced was nature itself. God first poured out his infinite love and beauty into very visible forms. Every part of His creation bears His divine footprint and fingerprint. His first incarnation of himself, came in the form of the universe. All of creation is actually love and beauty that's exploding outward in every direction. It's so natural for us to feel closer to God in nature! We are designed to enjoy and experience God in that way.

Visible creation is an outer form of beauty and wonder that points us to the inner formless Spirit, that is the inner source and energy for everything that we know and see.

"Creation is the primary and most perfect revelation of the Divine."
Thomas Aquinas

Creation is our first cathedral, our first place of worship and wonder.

Nature is the one song of praise that never stops singing. We were created to be aware of and read this book of creation, so we can know it's creator - the Author of life himself.

One of the many things we love about reading nature's Bible is that it points to cosmic companionship. It all points to a staggering Creator who also happens to be our father, who is the 24/7 organizing principle, generative love, limitless supply and meaningful purpose in it all.

Another thing we love about reading nature's Bible- the visible world- is that it also acts as a doorway to the spiritual world. The invisible world is so much larger than the material one. It points us to the mystery of incarnation. It shows us the essential union between the spiritual and material world - which is actually Christ himself.

When our outer world and our inner significance are experienced together, the result is a greater wholeness, joy, and beauty in our lives.

What Jesus personified was the manifestation of this important universal truth: Everything physical has always been the hiding place for everything spiritual. And we are daily invited to discover God there in fresh and new ways!

So how do we practice this?

Every time you are outside, become aware of some part of nature. Most of us rush around between appointments every day, feeling disconnected from God and our true identity, without actually noticing all of the divine invitations around us. Look around you and see what is 'calling' to you in the moment and is getting your attention. It could be: a flower; a tree; the wind; animals; clouds, etc. Stop and notice them for a few moments.

- *Read them.* What are they demonstrating about God? What beauty, energy, goodness, order, purpose, etc are they demonstrating or speaking that actually is pointing to God incarnating himself in that part of creation? What is it pointing to in you that is also him? Feel your union and connection with God in that moment.

- *Go outside at night.* When is the last time you really gazed at the sky at night, besides noticing if the moon is still there? Lay in your yard or go up on a roof or just sit in a chair for ten minutes and soak in the wonder of it all. If it's possible, go camping or drive to the outskirts of town where there is less light pollution so you can see even more stars.

- *Read them.* What are they demonstrating about God? What beauty, energy, goodness, order, purpose, etc. are they displaying that points you to God incarnating himself in that sky? What is it pointing to in you that is also in him? Feel your union and connection with God in that place.

- *Be intentional.* Go outdoors each week for the purpose of reading nature's Bible for a longer period of time. We promise that this can bring a different level of relaxation, love, and connection back into your life. Find a nature trail or park, lake, stream or garden. The difference between this extended time outdoors versus the momentary ones above, can be the difference between taking a quick shower or enjoying a long soak in the tub.

We regularly do this on our days off. Sometimes we ride our bikes. We live in a place where we can take our kayaks to the river, lake or ocean. We absolutely love going for hikes in state and national parks. There have been countless times we've taken lawn chairs to a quiet lake or river and sat there for several hours. Or we simply sit on our back porch and drink from the small simple fountain that nature offers us right there.

The point is to find several ways… that you enjoy… to easily access and experience your union with God through the created world. He is there in it all.

> *For since the beginning of the world the invisible attributes of God, e.g. his eternal power and divinity, have been plainly discernible through things which he has made and which are commonly seen and known…* **Romans 1:19 (Phillips Translation)**

Practice #2 - Get still and silent and alone with God.

"Be still and know that I am God."
Psalm 46:10

We know. That's a great verse but rarely do we dip into its waters because… either we can't seem to find the time OR when we do, it doesn't feel like anything really happens.

A recent study at the University of Virginia said that 67% of men and 25% of women would sooner endure an unpleasant electric shock rather than be alone in silence for fifteen minutes.

Blaise Pascal, the French philosopher and mystic said centuries ago: *"All human evil comes from this: our inability to sit still in a chair for half an hour."*

If you want to get serious at discovering and experiencing your wondrous, true identity, then this second practice is essential. We'd probably go so far as to say it's not even optional. It will move you from experiencing your self as a human doing to a true human being.

The Franciscan priest, Richard Rohr has said, *"You need to realize that all of reality starts in silence and later returns to silence. Everything first comes from nothing. That's why if you can find rest in the nothing, then you'll be prepared for the something. When nothing creates something, we call that grace."*

Jesus promised that there was *"a spring inside us-welling up unto eternal life"* (John 4:14). God is always found at the depths of things and in the depths it's always silent.

Avoiding silence is avoiding God and our true, created souls. Freedom begins with stopping our incessant thinking and judging of ourselves, others, and circumstances, and just becoming aware of something bigger within us.

Give yourself permission to relax your thinking and to let go of all your explanations about every part of life.

Loving silence is:

Holding impossibilities in a quiet embrace

Staying with mystery

Holding tensions

Absorbing contradictions

Smiling at paradox and inconsistency

Removing the distortions.

Max Picard in his book, *The World of Silence*, says: *"The human spirit requires silence just as much as the body needs food and oxygen."*

That's why the general spiritual rule is: The ego gets what it wants with words. And the soul finds what it needs in silence.

Awareness in silence and other such practices are simply to give us the ability to shift our identities from one to the other. It's intended to discover a larger truth, to discover a larger reality, to discover a larger self.

Here is one simple way we practice being still called: "Centering Prayer." It's been taught to Christians for centuries.

1. Sit comfortably with your eyes closed… breathing naturally… relax. Become aware of your love and desire for God in this moment, or even your lack of desire.

2. Now choose a word or phrase that expresses your intention to be open to God's presence (ex: "I'm here," "Just be", or "Grace, Rest, Father, Shepherd, Healer," etc.).

3. Hold the word gently, without speaking, repeating it in your mind slowly with the rhythm of your breathing.

4. Whenever you become aware of anything (thoughts, feelings, sensations, bills to pay), simply come back to internally saying your "word," which symbolizes your intention and desire for connection with God.

5. Gradually let the word fall away as you slip into silence. Rest there in silence of the loving presence of God.

6. Continue in silence as long as you wish – We suggest beginning with only five to ten minutes. (If you want, work up to twenty or more minutes twice daily as suggested by some teachers).

This is not practice to prove anything to God, yourself or to a spiritual leader. There is nothing whatsoever to prove in the presence of God. Nothing there to accomplish or "buy" - nothing to achieve. This is the practice of being your true self, sitting with God, enjoying that moment. You will still have needs but this practice invites you to experience the feeling of needing nothing more than this moment with God to feel whole.

I am who I am in the eyes of God. Nothing more. Nothing less.
St John of the Cross. 1579

Be at rest once more O my soul for the Lord has been good to you.
Psalms 116:7

Be still before the Lord and wait patiently for him.
Psalms 37: 8

He leads me beside still waters. He restores my soul.
Psalms 23: 2

The Lord your God is with you, he is mighty to save. He will take great delight in you He will quiet you with his love, he will rejoice over you with singing.
Zeph. 3:17

A prayer for living everyday from the Source of your true identity:

I put my trust in You today.

Lead me to Your arms.

Wash me in Your light.

Fill me with Your quietness.

Show me the irrelevancy of shadows-

of discontents and desires,

of resentments and idle thought-

of everything I think I made of myself apart from You.

Hold me and talk to me

until I see myself as You have seen me always,

until I know myself as You have known me forever,

until I find myself where I have never left,

bathed in Your joy, secure in Your love, at home, at rest, at one with You.

(From Spiritual Notes to Myself by Hugh Prather)

Acknowledgments & Thanks

We owe an immense debt of gratitude to so many who have come along side us, supported us, taught us, counseled us, and restored us. You have been Jesus to us and without your help this book would not have been possible.

These dear friends walked intrepidly through the most intense days of our lives and believed we would live to see another day. Thank you for not wavering in believing that God would somehow redeem our story: Francis & Susie Anfuso, Nancy & Warren Beach, Brian & Lorrie Ann Buckley, Kent & Lynn Shoemaker, Steve & Kristi Wells and Clark & Martha Whitten. We live forever in your debt.

We continue to learn from our counselors Dr. Rich Plass and Jim Cofield at crosspointministry.com. Their commitment to us; empathy for us; and revelations to us have changed our lives, and we don't think it's a stretch to say, they very possibly saved them. Their understanding of the Enneagram taught us to observe our patterns of being with unprecedented self clarity. Also, clinical psychologist Dr. Judy Johnson gave over a year of invaluable counsel, care and insight to Caron. We are forever grateful to God for her wisdom, kindness, continuing friendship and love.

Ruth Haley Barton and the Transforming Center's retreats for spiritual leaders (**http://transformingcenter.org**) first introduced us to the Enneagram and guided us in specific practices of silence in solitude and contemplative prayer. Her books *Strengthening the Soul of Your Leadership* and *Invitation to Silence and Solitude* prepared us for this journey and Ruth's personal care in our darkest days brought us great hope and comfort.

Mike Breen, Dave Rhodes, and Brandon Schaeffer at 3D Ministries first shared with us the concept of connecting the temptations in the garden to the temptations in the desert and how they tie into the core issues of all of our lives. Their concepts so resonated with what God was doing in us that it sparked a whole new series of insights. These men's passions for the mission of Christ and the openhearted way they received us when we lived among them for several months have forever marked us.

Richard Rohr of the Center for Action and Contemplation is a Franciscan priest, in his mid-70's, living in the desert of Arizona. His books, *The Enneagram: A Christian Perspective* and *Falling Upward* and others have provided deep insight, understanding and healing for our journey through "the desert" of the soul. Through the depth of his spiritual wisdom he became like a virtual pastor to us.

Grace Church of Orlando welcomed us into their spiritual community when ours was no longer available. The church and the leaders under pastor, Clark Whitten, and his wife, Martha, have exemplified the name of their church in heroic ways. They consistently walked with us and did not allow us to give up hope for our calling but encouraged us to prepare ourselves for a new day.

A group of church leaders and friemds who initiated and conducted a re-commissioning service for us in September 2014 told us God still wanted to use us and they wanted to affirm to the church community at large our emotional and spiritual health and viability. They will never know the life and hope this brought to us: Francis Anfuso, Nancy Beach, Paul & Mary Burleson, Jim Cofield, Joel Hunter, Bill Hybels, Danny Jones, Tom Lane, Richard & Debbie Lord, Scott & Claire Loughrige, David Smith, Clark & Martha Whitten.

A very special Sunday gathering of friends and families who have allowed us the privilege of testing much of the concepts in this book on them each week. Their eagerness to grow and learn as well as their care and support for us has been so very life giving. We are so deeply grateful for each of them.

Ami McCain. Ami is our virtual assistant who helped us in massive ways with the release of this book. When she found out what we were working on, she said she wanted to be involved. Her initiative, knowledge, experimentation, and flat out hard work helped make this happen. Ami is a rare gem and a huge gift from God to us.

And, above all, we are so deeply grateful to God for our remarkable sons Josh, Jon and Joe and their wives and children who have shown the ultimate courage, forgiveness and fortitude amidst unthinkable events and circumstances. We could not be where we are today without their deep love and desire to see past our failures to a much greater Truth.

About the Authors

David Loveless is a leadership coach, pastor to pastors, and strategic spiritual advisor to churches and businesses in over 50 countries. He is the co-founder of Live True Associates. He served as founding pastor of Discovery Church, Orlando, Fl for 29 years. During that time Discovery was identified in Dr. John Vaughn's book as one of "America's Most Influential Churches " and was named one of the Fastest Growing U.S. Churches in the 21stCentury by Outreach Magazine.

In the midst of enormous personal, family, and professional success, David also experienced devastating failure. Through rigorous personal work, prayer, and with the help of his wife, faithful friends and excellent counselors, the consequences of that experience have become his most life-defining teacher.

It is from this context of the highest high's and the lowest low's and with life-altering breakthroughs that sustain them today, David and his wife, Caron, feel privileged to offer their seasoned wisdom, experience, teaching, and transformational tools.

Caron Loveless is a bestselling author, artist, teacher, and co-founder of Live True Associates. She is a compassionate, intuitive coach, a certified Enneagram specialist and for over 25 years she used her strategic, leadership, and artistic gifts to serve on the executive staff at Discovery Church, Orlando, FL. She is a conference speaker and retreat leader with a passion to see women, couples and leaders identify the hidden, internal issues that hinder them from experiencing the maximum joy, grace and fulfillment God has for them.

Caron's art and books can be found at **hereugostudio.com**.

David and Caron are the parents of three adult sons, who along with their precious wives, have gifted them eight delightful grandkids.

Four ways you can continue to receive from David & Caron Loveless

1. Receive their free, practical, gut-honest blogs right to your inbox each week. They are passionate to pass on all the secrets they are learning to radically improve the way you see and experience your life, relationships and leadership.

2. They produce a weekly audio show called: "The Live True Podcast." You can listen to these at youlivetrue.com/live-true-podcast or subscribe via iTunes or your preferred podcast app on your digital device. Each episode is a dynamic conversation around proven and practical spiritual lessons that can revolutionize the way you see yourself, love and relate to others, and do your work with more fruitfulness & fulfillment.

3. They are available to speak at staff trainings; retreats, conferences, workshops and church services. They are eager to pass on practical, insightful, and transformational teaching that flows from decades of successful leadership as well as their own hard fought battles to see and live well from their ultimate identities.

4. They coach individuals, leaders, and couples as well as assess and consult with business and ministry teams.

They want to hear about your unique situation and help you determine the obstacles and design proven steps to overcome what is still blocking you, your marriage or your team from obtaining the deepest satisfaction and highest effectiveness possible.

How to contact David and Caron

Website: **youlivetrue.com**
David's email: **david@youlivetrue.com**
Caron's email: **caron@youlivetrue.com**
Facebook: **facebook.com/youlivetrue**

We Want To Hear From You!

We'd love to hear your thoughts, comments, or ways this book may have been helpful to you. You can contact David and Caron at any of the ways listed below:

Website: **youlivetrue.com**
David's email: **david@youlivetrue.com**
Caron's email: **caron@youlivetrue.com**
Facebook: **facebook.com/youlivetrue**

6-10-18
21-24
Mt. 26: 36-42

- Everyday we live our lives/circumstances on our preferences. Can we say YES to life even if it's not our preference?

- When we think the world revolves around me — move from NO to YES. (kayak - rocking chair)

- We try to avoid suffering at all cost. But there is suffering.
  1) Necessary Suffering - Life happens; No control
  2) Unnecessary suffering - When we resist it and try to fight it.

- Paul & Silas experienced an inner freedom before experiencing an external freedom. It's always an inside job first!! It starts / must start on the inside.
  Do you live in a prison cell?
  Go from "I prefer" to "I surrender", from NO to Yes. This brings freedom from within.
  Accept what is. This opens up a range of possibility. But when you refuse to accept what is happening then you only live in NO. — prison cell.